Ancient Egypt & Black Africa
A Student's Handbook for the Study of Ancient Egypt
in Philosophy, Linguistics & gender relations

Théophile Obenga

Edited by Amon Saba Saakana

Ancient Egypt & Black Africa
A Student's Handbook for the Study of Ancient Egypt
in Philosophy, Linguistics & gender relations

Théophile Obenga

Edited by Amon Saba Saakana

Translated from the French by Sylvianne Martinon and
Ahmed Sheik. This translation © 1992 Karnak House.

First published in Britain and the USA
by Karnak House
300 Westbourne Park Road
London W11 1EH
England

US office & distributors: Frontline International
751 East 75th Street
Chicago, Illinois 60619
USA

Fax: (312) 651.9850

Typesetting produced by Karnak Imagesetters

Printed by Whitehall Printers, Chicago & Naples, Florida

British Library Cataloguing in Publication Data

Obenga, Théophile

Ancient Egypt and Black Africa: A student's handbook for the study of
Ancient Egypt in philosophy, linguistics, and gender relations. —
Ancient Egyptian/African Classical Civilisation.
1. Egypt. History.
I. Title II. Saakana, Amon Saba 1948 — IV Series
932

ISBN 0-907015070-0

Very special thanks to Prof. Théophile Obenga who prepared the four
essays especially for the 5th annual conference of Afrikan Origin of
Civilization held at the School of Oriental and African Studies (London
University), October, 1990. Thanks also to Dr Louis Brenner for his co-
operation in staging the lectures at SOAS. The contributions of
Chukwunyere Kamalu and Ogonna Agu will appear later in a special
volume.

Dedicated to the author's wife
Yvonne Obenga

CONTENTS

FOREWORD

In the Realm of Knowledge:
Some notes on Kemit & Greece
Amon Saba Saakana   1/...

1. African Philosophy during the Period of the Pharaohs
                                                     18/...

2. African Origin of Philosophy   49/...

3. Genetic Linguistic Connections:
   Ancient Egypt & Black Africa   115/...

4. Male/Female relations in Ancient Egypt   163/...

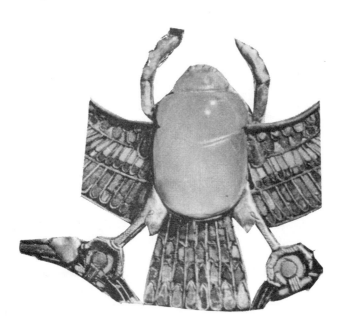

THE SCARAB

The scarab has immense symbolic meaning and significance
both in Egypt and Black Africa: The concept of
khepher ("to exist", "to become") is written with a hieroglyph
which is a sacred scarab. He is the One who creates the
Multiple. He is the first who engenders the others.
The scarab is also represented by the sun,
hieroglyphically
(pp. 38–9).

MATHEMATICS

For the ancient Egyptians mathematics (*rht, rekhet*, "number", "mathematics") deal with studying the entirety of nature, concrete reality as well as the enigmas and mysteries of the universe (p.43).

THE PHILOSOPHER

Under King Antef, from 2050 B.C., for the first time in history,
the philosopher is clearly defined in ancient Egypt. The
philosopher is the friend of wisdom. He is instructed,
and learns by studying nature. Philosophy is
therefore the exercise of *reason* in the fields
of the *relatedness* of thought and
action (p.56).

FOREWORD

IN THE REALM OF KNOWLEDGE: SOME NOTES ON KEMIT & GREECE

Amon Saba Saakana

The publication of this introductory volume of four lectures by Prof. Théophile Obenga marks a turning point in the methods and approaches in the study of comparative world history. This line was utilised by Cheikh Anta Diop in his multidisciplinary approach to the study of African history, and here advanced by his disciple, Théophile Obenga. What distinguishes Obenga's work from others is that he goes back to the original Greek in portraying the Greek world through the mouthpiece and language of their greatest thinkers. The fact that this approach, in relation to the precedence of Kemit (ancient Egypt) over that of the Greek world, has been consistently characterised as an expression of Greek misunderstanding, simultaneously, expresses the contradiction and the problematic of the spectre of Western civilization basing its traditional university education on that disseminated by the Greek model. Such a problematic never produces the obvious engagement of disentanglement. It merely increases the obligation of the Occident to degrade and underplay the significance of the development of scientific thought in Kemit - for which extant records of Greeks themselves confirm - which was only meaningfully propagated in Greece from the sixth century.

The publication of these essays which were specifically prepared by the author for the sixth annual conference of *The Afrikan Origin of Civilization*, held at the School of Oriental and African Studies (London University) at the beginning of the first week in October, 1990, demonstrated that mainstream academia had no stomach for debate, and, more importantly, felt that they could not debate with a highly qualified multidisciplinarian such as Théophile Obenga. It must be stated that weekly seminars are held at the Centre for African Studies in departments such as anthropology and area studies, and for which a visible number of the centre's academics regularly attend. The lectures were given a half-page exposure in the centre's termly bulletin, yet only two lecturers turned up. This demonstrated, if any further proof were needed, that any direction which veered away from the traditional monopoly of falsely proclaimed truth, would be ignored. It could not, and would not debate simply because such engagement led to validation of this tendency of difference and, consequently, could lead to valuing and interrogating such a position. Ignoring that it existed was the most effective method of disengagement. The consequence of such an action, however, opened the eyes of the students at the school which led, and will continue to lead, them into seriously interrogating the absence of debate and dialogue in an arena such as a university, which is supposedly an institution which teaches methodology, rationality, and the necessity to question.

Is there a Greek Philosophy?

Obenga engages this question with a rationality which has been too obvious for many scholars to have approached. In the essay, *The African Origin of Philosophy*, he anchors his questioning at the beginning by searching for an etymology of the word 'philosophy' and shows that its association with the word 'wisdom' does not stand up to scrutiny. He shows conclusively that the Greek vocabulary could not have developed this word. In support of Obenga's thesis, John Lyons, Professor of Linguistics and Dean of the School of Social Sciences at Sussex University, says:

Let us suppose, for example, that we are translating from Classical Greek into English and that we are confronted with the word 'sophia'. This is conventionally translated as 'wisdom'; and in many contexts this is, and more often might appear to be, a perfectly satisfactory equivalent. For example, let us consider a sentence containing the adjective 'sophos', related syntactically and semantically to 'sophia' as 'wise' is to 'wisdom', occurs in the Greek text in an author like Plato and is rendered into English as 'Homer is wiser than Hesiod'. Out of context, someone without either a good knowledge of Greek or a sufficient knowledge of the social and cultural background might well interpret this statement as if 'wise' were being used with the same meaning as it is in, say, 'Shakespeare was wiser than Marlowe'... But 'sophia' and 'wisdom' do not have the same range of meaning. In many contexts, the best English translation of the Greek sentence would be 'Homer is a better poet than Hesiod'. Indeed, it is arguable that this comes closest to what the Greek means when 'sophos' is being used in its **prototypical** sense. If a shoemaker or carpenter is good at his job, he is just readily called 'sophos' as a good doctor, poet or statesman is.[1]

It was necessary to produce this lengthy quote in order to see the development of contextual analysis advanced by the author which, uncategorically, places serious doubt on the mainstream interpretation of 'sophos', a component of *philosophia*. One could speculate that this knowingly carte blanche interpretation was probably motivated by political considerations, i.e., that it would advance Western civilization by placing wisdom in Greek antiquity. By posing such a seemingly rhetorical question one has opened up the debate on a fundamental notion of meaning: if a Greek philosophy existed, where is the Greek word which named such an intellectual activity? But the argument does not only hinge upon the etymology of the word philosophy, but on a number of connected claims which need to be vigorously interrogated.

Could Greek social life produce philosophy?

At the beginning of Greek cultural awakening, the society was already deeply rooted in a slave economy, i.e., the material gains from which the society was motored were derived from slave-owning. Therefore, at the time, in the seventh century, when Thales was reputed to have introduced philosophy into Greece, the society had a constitution which condoned slavery, usury, and the highly oppressive class system which would become the norm in Europe. Aristotle makes plain this fact:

> For the Athenian constitution was oligarchic in all other respects, and in particular the poor were enslaved to the rich — themselves and their children and their wives. All the land was in the hands of the few, and if the poor failed to pay their rents both they and their children were liable to seizure. All loans were made on the security of the person until the time of Solon: he was the first champion of the people. The harshest and bitterest aspect of aspect of the

constitution for the masses was the fact of their enslavement, though they were discontented on other grounds too: it could be said that there was nothing in which they had a share.[2]

Not only were the masses of people slaves, but the system of appointments to government reflected not a democracy but a despotism. This can be seen most vividly in the classification arranged by Solon, described by Aristotle as a 'champion of the people.' On attaining power, Solon classified the citizens into four distinct classes from the criteria of wealth:[3] the 500 bushel class if one can obtain from one's estate 500 measures of dry and liquid goods; the calvary if the measures were 300, the rankers whose measures should be 200, and the labourers who had no official office. From these classes came the officials of the state in gradations of importance. This was the basis of Western democracy right up to the beginnings of the 20th century when voting rights were based upon the possession of wealth and land ownership. This also highlights the problematic of Solon being projected as a liberator and yet confined in his political pragmatism to limiting the rights of the labouring classes to that of non-voters. One is not disputing that to both slaves and labourers in Athens Solon was a hero, but merely magnetising the fact of the limitation of participation in democratic Athenian life. This goes some way in explaining the social inequities constituted in Greek society and which clearly demonstrate the absence of any philosophical school which disputed that of the state.

Even the convinced moralist, Socrates, did not experience a conflict of conscience by exonerating the murder of a labourer by a landed proprietor. In *Euthyphro*, the character of the same name informs Socrates that he was prosecuting his own father for manslaughter. Socrates responds with shock:

Socrates: Good heavens! Of course, most people have no idea, Euthyphro, what the rights of such a case are. I imagine that it isn't everyone that may take such a course, but only one who is far advanced in wisdom.

Euthyphro: Far indeed, Socrates.

Socrates: Well, is the person that your father has killed a member of your own household? — Obviously he is; you wouldn't, of course, be prosecuting him for killing an outsider. [4]

Socrates constructs a debate, an argument, a rationale for the justification of the labourer's murder and the exoneration of Euthyphro's father. This goes on for several pages until, finally, Socrates produces his masterpiece of moral reasoning:

Socrates: ...If you didn't know all about piety and impiety you would never have attempted to prosecute your aged father for manslaughter on behalf of *a mere labourer*, you would have been too much afraid of the gods, and too much ashamed of what men might think, to run such a risk, in case you should be wrong in doing so... [5] (emphasis added)

Interestingly, although Socrates' dialogues, laced with the double entendre and innuendo, attempt to dissuade Euthyphro from prosecuting his father, Euthyphro leaves precisely at the time of Socrates' intransigence. Comparatively, this lack of responding to confrontation is a dictum of Kemit, enshrined in the *Instructions of King Amenemope*. The question can now be posed whether one can seriously attribute the title of philosopher to Socrates who demonstrates no reservation in weighing the murder of a labourer (the lowest class) against a probable hostile response from the public. Here Socrates does not exhibit any of the qualities of 'philosopher' in moral terms which we can understand: murder is murder whether committed by a slave or a king, but for Socrates, and for Greece, there was a clear distinction in the act of murder based upon class. This can be traced and compared to the Greek canon in morality which Tobin shows does not allow for moral distinction in wrong or right, but only in the defence of status: '...▲ikh functions solely to maintain an established *status quo*, with no consideration as to whether it be right or wrong in a moral sense.' [6] It can be deduced, therefore, that although Socrates was launching himself into an unacceptable moral and philosophical domain, foreign to the Greek established canon (and to the Athenian state), he was both contradictory and affirmatory. That is to say, that he was still physically confined to Greece and its environment of influence, yet connected to a philosophical system (Kemitan) which animated his sense of morality to introduce a new canon to the Greek world. That he died for such a defence is admirable, but that the contradictions in his life were apparent, testify to a veritable conflict of moral and social interests.

The Cretan Epimenides who counselled Solon prior to the latter taking office, schooled the Athenians in 'abolishing the cruel and barbarous customs' of their women and that they should be 'more observant of justice and more inclined to union.'[7] Elsewhere, in detailing the story of Atlantis, Plato's narrator refers to 'the various barbarian and Greek nations of the day...'[8] It should be noted that Greece was not a unified nation at this stage, but consisted of ethnic groups and separate towns within a single land mass. Solon who abandoned Athens for Kemit after the hostility expressed to his reforming policies and subsequently spent ten years there, was firstly influenced by Kemitan laws in instituting new policies in Greece.[9] But Plato in *Timaeus* positively points to Solon's education in Kemit *prior* to his short reign in office. Critias says, '...if he had finished the story he brought back from Egypt, and hadn't been compelled to neglect it because of the class struggles and other evils he found here on his return...'[10] So that one sees that even in the basic introduction of humanising laws, for the first time in Greece, Kemit played the fertilising role model. That

Solon had to flee Athens in his return to Egypt testifies to the social circumstances which prevailed in Greece at this time which made social egalitarianism a veritable impossibility.

What was the meaning of the Sage in Greece?

According to the editors of Plutarch's *Lives*, 'The first sages were in reality great politicians, who gave rules and precepts for the government of communities. Thales was the first who carried his speculations into physics.'[11] Obenga's essay carries too much elaboration for further comment on Thales, but the fact that this is openly admitted by the educational establishment testifies to the fact that Greece did not produce philosophers up to this time. The editors extend their comments to the sophists who were '...rather rhetoricians than philosophers, skilled in words, but superficial in knowledge, as Diogenes Laertius informs us. Protogoras (sic), who flourished about the eighty-fourth olympiad, a little before the birth of Plato, was the first who had the appellation *Sophist*. But Socrates, who was more conversant in morality than in politics, physics, or rhetoric, and who was desirous to improve the world rather in practice than in theory, modestly took the name of *Philosophos* , i.e. *a lover of wisdom* , and not that of *Sophos*, i.e. *a sage or wise man*.'[12]

One readily understands the admission of the non-Greek sources for the concept of philosopher. This is not only supported by critical reasoning but by facts.

Socrates, reputed to be one of the greatest Greek thinkers, while awaiting his condemnation in prison because of his moral stance on corrupt Greek civil life, admitted that he was writing fables from the work of Aesop, the Ethiopian philosopher whose wisdom has come down to us in the form of fables: '..I availed myself of some of Aesop's fables which were ready to hand and familiar to me, and I versified the first of them that suggested themselves.'[13] The King of Lydia, Croesus, had Aesop at his court and 'caressed him not a little.'[14] This is taken to mean that Croesus paid great attention to Aesop and treated him respectfully in order for him to remain. The Greeks, by comparison, according to de Lubicz, were prone to 'contradict, and to argue' which has always been 'part of the intelligent and subtle temperament of the Greek.'[15] This predilection for argument, debate, contradiction rather than knowledge and conviction, is clearly and repeatedly demonstrated in *Phaedo* where Socrates talks for hours in his attempt to convince his fellow "philosophers" on the existence of the soul. This debate is touched on intermittently but persistently throughout the length of Plato's dialogue. This confirms the fact that as late as Socrates' and Plato's time the concept of the soul surviving death was not accepted in Greece. Socrates' argument for affirming his belief is obviously predicated upon his acquisition of knowledge in Kemit (although Socrates is reputed not to have ever left Greece, the opposite is detailed by Obenga). Socrates continuously registers the disbelief and doubt of his companions, '...if you feel any difficulty about our discussion, don't hesitate to put forward your own views...'[16] That the concept of the philosopher as a general appellation in the Greek world was not accepted cannot be disputed. The fact that in the Kemitan context philosophy, according to Obenga, was a vocation consisting of a knowledge of all the sciences: mathematics, physics, astronomy, medicine, etc., and that this did not appear in Greece until Thales in the seventh century and Pythagoras in the sixth, when these subjects were rigidly taught in the Kemitan temples in deep antiquity.

This line of reasoning is not unique to Socrates but to several other Greeks. Plato, in discussing the possible transformation of the Greek ruler, Dionysius of Greater Greece (Sicily) from a tyrant to a ruler of conscience, still applied the criterion of property ownership as an index of qualification for membership of an imagined ruling council: first the 'best' men should be drawn from a 'long and honourable descent', each possessing 'an adequate amount of property.'[17] In a crucial comparative sense, Plato's philosophical thoughts upon politics, i.e., the reforming of a tyrant through the light of conscience and reason, predates the Fabians who were firmly committed to participating in British colonial life, infiltrating key government positions with the illusion of eventual transformation. For the Fabians, this plot was a failure, and for Plato it too was a failure. Although the public conscience eventually accommodated the fact of the slaves' revolution, the foundation upon which democracy rested: the exploitation of the majority by the minority, continued unabated. Dionysius, needless to say, remained a tyrant.

Under these harsh materialist facts it would have been impossible for Greece to have produced philosophers. The materialist foundation upon which the society's mode of production was based was that of slavery and the accommodation of oppression, sanctioned in the constitution and in social life, which rendered any significant changes to Greek society impossible. This is certainly not the case in Kemit where there was no private ownership of land, where capital punishment was absent, where the death of a person, whether peasant or king, could result in serious judicial consequences, where the mode of production, communalistic rather than individualistic, alienated the possibility of the cult of individuality and of wealth from becoming a reality. It is precisely the opposite with the Greeks: upon winning control of the Kemitan state they immediately forced the population into labour, deprived them of communal ownership, opened banks in the most remote villages, and corrupted the matriarchal basis of the society through murder to that of patriarchy and oppression.[18]

Additionally, a crucial understanding of the transmission of knowledge can be understood by the

direct line that the Greek educational lineage inherited from Kemit. Let us note the following:
1. 'Thales was the first true philosopher...Pythagoras visited Thales in Miletus...Pythagoras was apt to sit at home singing paens of praise to Thales...Thus he recommended that Pythagoras go to Egypt in order to learn the same secrets from the priests as he had once done when a young man.'[19]
2. In Pythagorean circles, secrecy was paramount, thus 'Hippasos revealed the properties of the dodecahedron and was expelled from the society. Empedokles learnt all he could from being a member of the society, then left it to write his famous poems full of Pythagorean lore...Pythagoras demanded a vow of secrecy concerning his doctrines. In the fifth century B.C. also Philolaus (it is rumoured, because he needed the money) wrote his fascinating books which were purchased by Plato, who, in turn embodied these Pythagorean beliefs in his own works...in the third century A.D. Iamblichus and Porphyry sought to rehabilitate his (Pythagoras') reputation by showing most of the developments in Platonic and other philosophy were due to him... Ammonius of Alexandria, the teacher of Plotinus and hence of Porphyry, who was in turn the teacher of Iamblichus.'[20]

This clearly shows that there was a direct line of educational lineage from Thales, seventh century B.C. to the third century A.D. This line was extended during the Italian and European Renaissance which renovated mundane European thought which had for centuries been encased within Christian dogma and heresy. The Renaissance unleashed a new version/vision of ancient Greece in which, by the nineteenth century, the historical genesis of invented traditions — which made one attach oneself to questionable genealogies — were extended to deny the fundamental influence of Kemit. Greece became the incubator for Western science, art and philosophy. But a fundamental error was made in this claim: the concomitant *social system was inimical to the development of humanity*. Instead philosophy, like immoral science itself, became attached to tyrannical governments. The fact that the Western educational system did not perceive of the ritual of initiation which would guarantee the moral perfectibility of humanity before admission to the higher phases of scientific knowledge can only be understood from the materialist proclivities of the societies themselves. Accomplishment was the goal, not the greater good which so inoculated the sacerdotal colleges of Kemit. The omission and consequence of such ignorance continue to plague the world with wars, nuclear disasters, ecological catastrophes, and the class system. So that any advance in science and education was placed in the hands of democratic tyrants: whether Hitler or Stalin, Thatcher or Reagan. True philosophy could never have been achieved in a society in which the king/president/prime minister was never anchored in the ethics of cosmic thought.

Herein lies the basis of continuing conflict in the modern world: moral thought is disseminated only as an ideal, never as pragmatism. It could not be otherwise since the material base of the society, the mode of production, necessarily militated against the development of true religiosity, spirituality and morality. Obenga achieves an original insight into the compared states of Greece and Kemit: the information contained in these four essays are sufficient to inflame the curiosity of the earnest student of African civilizations to launch him/herself into further and deeper exploration. These essays are essential guidelines for the study of Kemit and, by extension, the whole of Africa and the Indo-European world.

REFERENCES

1. John Lyons, *Language and Linguistics,* Cambridge University Press, 1981, pp.325/6.
2. Aristotle, *The Athenian Constitution,* trans. P.J. Rhodes, Penguin, Middlesex, 1984, p.43.
3. Ibid, pp.48-9.
4. Plato, *The Last Days of Socrates (Euthyphro),* trans. Hugh Tredennick, Penguin, Middlesex, 1954, p.22.
5. Ibid, p.41.
6. Vincent Arieh Tobin, "*Ma^{C}at and* ▲*IKH: Some Com-*

Comparative Consideration of Egyptian and Greek Thought," in Journal of the American Research Center in Egypt, Vol. 24, 1987, p.114.
7. Plutarch's *Lives*, trans. J. Langhorne/W. Langhorne, George Routledge & Sons, London, n.d., p.64.
8. Plato, *Timaeus and Critias*, trans. Desmond Lee, Penguin, Middlesex, 1965, p.131.
9. Plutarch, op. cit., p.68.
10. Plato, op. cit., p.34.
11. Plutarch, op. cit., p.85.
12. Ibid.
13. Plato, *The Last Days of Socrates (Phaedo)*, p.103.
14. Plutarch, op. cit., p.71.
15. R.A. Schwaller de Lubicz, *Sacred Science*, Inner Traditions International, New York, 1982, p.18.
16. Plato, op. cit., p.137.
17. Plato, *Phaedrus and Letters VII and VIII*, trans. Walter Hamilton, Penguin, Middlesex, 1973, p.130.
18. For a discussion of these ideas, see H. Riad, "*Egypt in the hellenistic era,*" in G. Mokhtar, ed., *General History of Africa 11, Ancient Civilizations of Africa, Paris*, London, California, Unesco, Heinemann, University of California Press, 1981.
19. Peter Gorman, *Pythagoras A Life*, Routledge & Kegan Paul, London, 1979, pp.25, 35.
20. Ibid, p.118.
21. For a profound and penetrating analysis of the differences in the Greek/European and African modes of production, see Cheikh Anta Diop, *Civilization or Barbarism*, Lawrence Hill, N.Y., 1991.

1.

AFRICAN PHILOSOPHY DURING THE PERIOD OF THE PHARAOHS

1. The Question of "African Philosophy"

These are just comments and introductory remarks in order to avoid all sorts of confusions, and to determine our subject more accurately.

By "philosophy", both loosely and exactly, we mean speculations which concern human destiny and condition. Such speculations or reflections lead to problems such as the creation or advent of the world, problems such as freedom, the immortality of the soul, the existence of God, the knowledge of thoughts, feelings and actions of man, sciences, their object and their method, beauty (esthetics), what is

ANKHENATEN

In Ankhenaten's *Great Hymn to Aton*
one sees more than a text of monotheism and expression of
faith. It reveals an exact knowledge of nature
which is surprisingly scientifically precise when
compared to modern scientific
knowledge (p. 41).

good, moral, virtuous, and what is true. Such speculations or reflections are obviously to be distinguished from common, vulgar opinions (the Greek *doxa*); they must be conscious of themselves, that is to say, at least self-explanatory.

Before the present comprehension of the word "philosophy", we had started by including under this term all of human knowledge, then some of them, little by little, were formed into independent disciplines: mathematics, astronomy, physics, chemistry, biology, history, geography, etc. Philosophy was therefore the study of Nature, in the greatest sense of the word: natural Nature, social Nature, human Nature.

Aristotle, for example, studied all these sciences, all this knowledge.

The supreme aim of such speculations and such knowledge was for humankind to acquire wisdom (*sophia* in Greek): wisdom is born of science, of knowledge, and, etymologically, in the Greek language, the word "philosophy" supposedly means: "love of wisdom".

Philosophical speculations can present themselves either in oral form, that is to say, the oral statement (Socrates), or in the written form, that is to say, in the written statement (Plato, Aristotle). What is important and essential is that such speculations should be expressed explicitly.

One can therefore acknowledge, *a priori*, that there are, in black Africa, speculations and philosophies, in oral and written forms. But such speculations and philosophies can only be proved posteriorly, that is to say, "discovered", extracted from their form of transmission, and studied after research work (cf. *Conversations with Ogotomeli* by Marcel Griaule, Oxford University Press, on the Dogon of Mali).

This research work is, at the same time, of an historic, linguistic and philosophical order:

* *History* allows one to determine the period and the chronological frame of African speculations and philosophies;

* *Linguistics* are a way of taking these and other semiotic means into account to relate these philosophies in a given society;

* *Philosophical method* allows one to question and exploit to the fullest speculations and philosophies, in order to extract from their contents, the fundamental concepts, the human message, the ultimate significance.

One can see that to talk about African philosophy, one must get away from the well trodden paths of Africanist studies which are often unaware of the temporal dimension of the studied societies, of the linguistic and semiological means of these societies.

On the other hand, the very richness of European philosophy in Greece and Rome in antiquity, then over the course of the centuries, in France, in Germany, in Great Britain, in Italy, made us unaware, more or less up to recently, of African philosophies or those of India or China.

In Africa, because of cultural prejudices, Africanists, that is to say, Europeans who study African civilizations, obviously from the outside, admit on the whole the existence of "systems of thought", "cosmogonies", "visions of the world", etc., but never of "philosophy" in black Africa. The most daring of these Africanists mention "ethnophilosophy", going a step further than Lucien Lévy-Bruhl (1857 - 1939) and his "prelogism". Others suggest the term "pre-philosophy", gratuitously suggesting that true philosophy starts with ancient Greece.

Well, today, thanks to the work of African scholars especially in Cameroon, Benin, Ghana, Nigeria, Senegal, Zaire and Kenya, it is now established that there are African philosophies which can be studied and taught even when compared to philosophical speculations compiled elsewhere in the world, in Europe, in Asia, in America.

But this very important work of African graduate philosophers only concern the modern and contemporary period, for example, from Anton Wilhelm Amo (18th century) to today (with Kwame Nkrumah, author of *Consciencism*).

Therefore, one must try to fill the temporal gaps by undertaking thorough research in order to re-establish the whole history of African philosophy from antiquity to the present. This is why we are interested in African philosophy of the Pharaonic period: to connect the contemporary with that of the ancient and to demonstrate the pre-existence of African ph015osophy before its appearance anywhere else on this earth.

2. African Philosophy during the period of the Pharaohs: Questions of method and documentation

An initiation into general philosophy is necessarily prescribed, for such an initiation allows us to understand how the task of studying philosophy is undertaken and what the very object of philosophical thought is.

In our case, we were initiated into the history of Western philosophy from the Greek thinkers to contemporary philosophers, at the University of Bordeaux in France. The particular history of ancient Egypt must also be known in its essential characteristics and moments, as much as the Egyptian Pharaonic language. It is in fact useful to try to understand the ancient Egyptian world from the inside, instead of contenting oneself with works, however erudite, which do not always exploit all the available information.

For a long time, Egyptologists have been trying to understand Egyptian thought. Let us point out some of the most meaningful:

* James H. Breasted, *The Development of Religion and Thought in Ancient Egypt*, New York, Scribner's, Harper's, 1972.

* John A. Wilson, *Egypt: The nature of the Universe*, chap II, pp.31 - 61.

* John A. Wilson, *Egypt: The Function of the State*, chap III, pp. 62 - 92.

* John A. Wilson, *Egypt: The Values of Life*, chap IV, pp.93 - 22.

These three beautiful studies by Wilson can be found in the collective work: *The Intellectual Adventure of Ancient Man*, Chicago, 1946, 1977.

* Erik Hornung, *Les Dieux de l'Egypte, Le un et le Multiple* (in German *Der Eine und die Vielen*, 1971), Monaco, Editions du Rocher, 1986.

In this important work, Professor Hornung from the University of Bâle lays down some of the tenets of ancient Egyptian philosophy: the oneness of God, the greatness and the transcendence of God, the divine action and the human response.

＊ Jan Assmann, *Maât, l'Egypte pharaonique et l'idée de justice sociale*, Paris, 1989. Conférences essais et leçons du Collège de France.

Professor Jan Assman of the University of Heidelberg, studies carefully and precisely in this essay, the structures of ancient Egyptian thought and social organisation, supported by the actual wisdom texts of the Egyptians.

There were many studies on "Egyptian religion", to such an extent that it is common to speak more of religion than of philosophy, when it comes to Egypt.

Here are the titles of some synthesised works on "Egyptian religion":

＊ A. Erman, *La religion des Egyptiens* (available in English as *Egyptian Religion*), translated from German, Paris, Payot, 1952, with 1 map, 57 diagrams and 53 plates.

＊ H. Frankfort, *Ancient Egyptian Religion: An Interpretation*, Columbia University, 1948, with 31 illustrations.

＊ G. Jéquier, *Considérations sur les religions égyptiennes*, Neuchâtel, La Baconnière,1946, with 101 diagrams.

＊ S.A.B. Mercer, *The Religion of Ancient Egypt*, London, Luzac & Co., 1949.

＊ S. Morenz, *La religion égyptienne. Essaii d'interprétation*, translated from German, Paris, Payot, 1962. This is the most recent work.

＊ J. Sainte Fare Garnot, *La vie religieuse dans l'ancienne Egypt*, Paris, PUF, 1948.

＊ J. Vandier, *La religion égyptienne*, Paris, PUF, 1949.

＊ Ph. Virey, *La religion de l'ancienne Egypte*, Paris, Gabriel Beauchesne & Cie, 1910, with 21 diagrams.

In most of these synthesised works on Egyptian religion, we find developments on the creation or the advent of the world, on Egyptian religious concepts such as Maât, on the Egyptian concept of divinity, on Egyptian ideas of death and the beyond. The last chapter of the above mentioned work by A. Erman on Egyptian religion, treats the expansion of Pharaonic religion in Europe: god, morality, philosophy, temples, sculptures, worship, festivals, and mysticism.

Regarding Egyptian documentation itself, it is now available, texts and translations, in most European languages (German, English, Italian, French, Spanish, Russian, Dutch). They concern texts written by the ancient Egyptians themselves which, luckily, have come down to us. Here are the titles of the main ones which might interest anyone who is into "Egyptian Philosophy", in chronological order:

Ancient Empire (2815 - 2400 BC)

＊ *The Pyramid Texts:* a corpus of 2217 formulae or paragraphs in modern editions; these formulae are inscribed on the inside walls of the chambers of the Kings' pyramids, sometimes of the Queens', from the fifth dynasty (Ounas, around 2600 BC). It is an important legacy of ancient Egypt, and one can find fragments of the texts on funerary monuments of the saite period (around 600 BC).

＊ *Teachings or Wisdoms or Instructions*: these are sapiential works which convey a humanism, suggesting to Man the route to honest conduct and to success: *Teachings of Imhotep*, adviser to King Djoser (3rd dynasty, around 2800 BC), doctor and architect of the graded pyramid of Saqqara;

* *The Teachings of Hordjedef*, second son of Chéops (4th dynasty, c.2700 BC);

* *The Teachings for Kagemni*, vizier of Snefrou (4th dynasty), Snefrou's vizier (4th dynasty); *The Teachings of Ptah-hotep*, vizier under the reign of Isesi (5th dynasty, c.2600 BC); *The Teachings of Kairès* are less known. Only *The Teachings of Ptah-hotep* reached us in its totality, thanks to more recent copies. These teachings are a remarkable type of research into moral perfection (because "nobody was born wise"), and also a search for refined language.

The text called *Memphite theology* transmitted by the stele of Shabaka, is an essay on philosophical and theological reflection of Ptah's priests in his Memphis sanctuary. This essay on cosmogony and theogony refers to the "speech" (language) and the "thought" (heart) of Ptah, the creator of all that exists: god, man, quadrupeds, reptiles.

First Intermediate Period (9th - 11th dynasties: 2300 - 2050 BC)

* *Admonitions of an Egyptian Sage* ("Ipuwer's prophecies"): this work reveals a huge effort of literary research (birth of poetic art in Egypt) in speaking of the sad effects of the political and social changes which occurred in the country.

* *Dialogue of a desperate person and his/her ba* ("soul"): a desperate man discusses with his soul (with himself) on the opportunity of staying in the world of the living, from where are now banished the values which made it attractive.

* *The Teachings for King Merikarê*, attributed to King Khety II (Akhtoes: 10th dynasty): it is a treaty of good political and moral conduct with reflections on personal attitudes to justice, meditative silence, respect for the laws, fear of God, preparation for a happy destiny in the beyond, and on the equilibrium they can bring to society.

* *Songs of the harpist*: poems sung by singers, in funerary scenes, where a blind harpist plays his instrument (the first example known of these songs is the one engraved on King Antef's tomb: 11th dynasty, around 2100 BC); the essential theme is the inscrutability of the mystery of death.

* *Tale of the Oasian* (the "loquacious peasant"): one of the longest literary texts of ancient Egypt, where a peasant of the oasis (Ouadi Natroum, west of the Delta), ill-treated by the men of a local unscrupulous official, complains to superior authorities, up to the king himself. The plaintiff approaches, in nine discourses, the usual themes of wisdom: conception of the authorities' duties, rights of the poor, importance of justice in the eyes of gods and men, etc.

Middle Empire (2000 - 1800 BC)

* *The Teaching of Amenemhat to his son Sêsostris:* here is a pessimistic vision of the world where the good people are caused unpleasantness: whoever trusts their friends is betrayed by them.

* *Satire of trades,* the work of Khety, "son of Douaouf": the importance of this composition lies in the detailed and satirical description of various manual trades (blacksmith, carpenter, barber, potter, shoemaker) which enables us to get an idea of social and artisanal life of the time. The only profession which appears to be noble and appealing is the profession of scribe: it is an eulogy of intellectual life in ancient Egypt.

* *Tales of the Westcar Papyrus:* the fourth tale is very instructive. King Chéops asks the magician Djedi: "Is it true Djedi, that you can put back a chopped head?" After Djedi's affirmative answer, the King commands: "Bring the prisoner from prison after his execution". And Djedi answers: "No, not a human being, my master and King, because it is forbidden to do such a thing to God's sacred flock". But Djedi will succeed with two geese and an ox. Capital punishment does not seem to have existed in ancient Egypt, that is, for the country's subjects.

* *The Sarcophagus Texts* (end of the 11th dynasty, 12th dynasty): the orientation of these texts written on the surface of sarcophagus is the same as on the texts of the pyramids of the Ancient Empire: it is always about giving the dead the benefits of a happy immortality thanks to the Osirian mysteries. These texts are therefore formulae of revitalization through the union of the deceased with a divinity: it was said that each part of the mummified corpse belonged to a god.

New Empire (1590 - 1085 BC)

* *The Book of the Dead* : these are texts on papyri

illustrated with vignettes placed near the dead in coffers. The Egyptians refer to it as "The Book of Coming Forth by Day". This title is written inside the scroll with the formulas placed at the dead's disposal. It is a compilation of formulas: 192 chapters in modern editions. These formulas date back from the 18th dynasty to the 26th dynasty (around 600 BC). These formulas allow the deceased to be united to the sun which at night, travels through the sky (the "Douat") and to join it again at daybreak. One must mention Chapter 125, commonly called "The Negative Confessions" or "The Declaration of Innocence", which partly reflects a moral ideal already present in funerary inscriptions of some high ranking officials in the ancient Empire. The admirable vignette which ornates this chapter in "The Papyrus of Ani" depicts a scene of "psychostasia" or "thought of the heart".

 * *The Great Hymn to Aton*, kept in the tomb of one of Akhenaton's officials, Ay: the literary and philosophical value of this document has been emphasised many times. This hymn to Aton contains precious speculations on nature.

 * *The Wisdom of Ani*: advice on prayer, good education, behaviour with women, education of children, preparation for death.

 * *The Teachings of Amenemope*: 30 chapters ("notices") with the same preoccupation as Ani's, with perhaps a stronger emphasis on the respectful behaviour of the person, and a more delicate religious

meaning.

Late period (21st - 30th dynasties: 1000 - 332 BC)

* Inscriptions on the *Tomb of Pétosiris* and his family (around 300 BC): in these, one finds the highest expression of sapiential and sacerdotal spirituality: eulogy of the holy life of a man who follows the will of God. This overview is obviously very brief. The literary production of ancient Egypt stretches to almost 3000 years. But it is necessary to refer to Egyptian texts themselves, to read them directly, and to exploit them to the fullest. Anthologies are available to those who have no direct access to the Egyptian language:

* A. Erman, *The Literature of the Ancient Egyptians. Poems, Narratives and Manuals of Instructions*, from the third and second millennia BC, translated into English by Aylward M. Blackman, New York, 1971; first published 1927.

* W.K. Simpson, *The Literature of Ancient Egypt, An Anthology of Stories, Instructions, and Poetry*, new edition, New Haven, Yale University Press, 1973.

* M. Lichtheim, *Ancient Egyptian Literature*, Vol 1: *The Old and Middle Kingdoms* (1973, 1975); Vol 2: *The New Kingdom* (1976); Vol 3: *The Late Period* (1980), Los Angeles, University of California Press.

* Cl. Lalouette, *Textes sacrés et textes profanes de l' ancienne Egypte*, 2 Vols., Paris, Gallimard,1984 - 1987.

* G. Lefebvre, *Romans et contes égyptiens de l'époque pharaonique*, Paris, Adrien-Maisonneuve,1949.

3. Some concepts and themes of Egyptian Philosophy

Having defined what is understood by "philosophy", and precisely "African philosophy", after going over the methodological demands for any study of African philosophy, after stressing the importance of Pharaonic philosophy in the chronological, global context of the history of African philosophy (and of the world), and after briefly stating the documentation (studies, syntheses, anthologies) related to African philosophy, it is now time to try and highlight a few concepts and themes of this African philosophy of the Pharaonic period.

(a) *The Egyptian concept of the world before the world and the advent of the world as we know it*

The world as it is now: heavens, earth, stars, planets, vegetation, animals, man, life, death, civilization, is the work of God, or of the Demiurge-Creator. Hence, at the beginning of beginnings, there is God. God is before the world. The world is created by God. There isn't a "world before" or a something, whatever, before God. Almost all religions and known cosmogonies hold to this vision, which put the creator, God, before anything that exists: light, darkness, the constituting elements of the universe, the universe itself in its totality and its globality. Thus Saint Augustine, for instance, explains that the mass of the world (*universa mundi moles*): the sun, the moon, the stars, the sky, the earth, the birds, terrestrial animals, the water, the fishes, man, in short, all that exists, is truly the work of God, but God did not create his works (*opera*) from nothing (*ex nihilo*), nor from matter foreign to him or previous to him (*non de aliqua non tua vel quae antea fuerit*), but from concreated matter (*concreata*), that is to say, from matter created simultaneously (*simul*) by God. The original matter from which God will operate is not previous to God, nor to his creatures: this original matter is created like the creatures are created, by the operational divine force (St. Augustine, *Confessions*, Book 13, 48: "*De nihilo enim a te, non de te facta sunt, non de aliqua non tua vel quae antea fuerit, sed de concreata, id est simul a te creata materia*").

Saint Augustine's explanation is evidently idealist, just as the biblical explanation of the genesis of the world.

A very different schema appears with the explanation of the advent of the world by Egyptian philosophers. For ancient Egypt, before the world such as it is, before the sky, the earth, men, before death, before the gods themselves, before what was to be should come to exist (*n sep kheperet semen ti*), there was something: the *Noun*.

The *Noun* is not really definable. It is a state of the world or the matter before everything which constitutes the Universe. The *Noun* is before the Universe, before the gods, before the sky, before the earth, before death, before the death of the Pharaoh himself, before the anterior gods who will create the world such as it is now.

This primordial *Noun* can be related to the abysmal water, but it is more like a fluid ether, and not real water. This fluid, liquid ether is the generator of the gods themselves, and of the rest of creation. This *Noun* is uncreated. Everything created emerges from the *Noun*, including the gods themselves. There is not a "Creator God" independent from primordial matter. Conversely, the primordial matter is before the Creator God. The Creator God will emerge of his own force from the initial *Noun*, uncreated. The *Noun* is the initial non-created, the cosmic before, the universe before, the universe before the actual universe. This uncreated, fluid, etherised liquid, very opaque, dense, compact, will be involved in the Demiurge through the process of becoming — the demiurge himself issued from this primordial uncreated.

We are now commenting on *The Pyramid Texts* (1040, 1230, 1466): God is born in the *Noun:* "When I was born in the *Noun*" (*msi.i m Nnw);* "I am Atoum, when I alone exist, being alone in the *Noun*" (*ink Itm m w ^{C} m wn w ^{C}r.k m Nnw*); "It is *Noun,* father of the gods" (*Nnw nw it.f ntrw*).

So the *Noun* gives form to the primitive world of the Creator Gods, themselves emerging from the *Noun.* "I created in the *Noun,* when I was still somnolent" (*ts.n.i im m Nnw m nni*). One can read this in the *Bremner Papyrus.* The *Noun* is truly what is primordial and from which everything will exist. The gods, the sky, the earth, all living beings, in short, the global world, visible and invisible. The *Noun* is the Cause, the Reason, the Foundation, the Principle. From the *Noun,* there is being, development, knowledge. The *Noun* is the foundation and the home of all subsequent becoming. The *Noun* is anterior to that which is subsequent: it is the *before,* and the *after* will emerge out of this uncreated *before.*

The Demiurge reigns alone, unique in this primordial uncreated. The Demiurge creates from the uncreated from which he also comes.

This explanation of the genesis of the world is still present today in many black African societies. Here is a philosophical text from the Kuba of Kasai (Zaire), quite comparable to the Egyptian texts: "At the beginning, there was nothing but darkness, and there was nothing but water on earth. In this chaos, Bumba, the Chembe, reigned alone. First he vomited the sun, then the moon, and then the stars: this is how light was born", etc... (E. Torday and T.A. Joyce, *Notes Ethnographiques sur les Peuples communément appellés Bakuba*, Bruxelles,1910, p.20).

Hence this comparative chart:

Ancient Egypt	Kuba of Zaire
1. The *Noun,* primordial water, before all creation: matter not yet organised	1. *Liquid chaos* (primordial water) before all creation: matter not yet organised
2. Ra, Atoum is *alone* , still somnolent in the *Noun*	2. Bumba the Chembe (God), is *alone* in the liquid chaos
3. Ra, Atoum creates: the creator sun.	3. Bumba the Chembe, first creates light: the creator sun.

With this concept of the *Noun,* the Egyptian philosophers laid down a principle (*archè* in Greek) at the source of the very constitution of the Universe as it is now known by human ingenuity. Also, it lays down, quite clearly, the radical unity of all the beings and elements of the universe, issued and created from a unique principle — a kind of fluid ether. According to the philosophical school of Miletus, founded by Thales, a former pupil of Egyptian priests, the ultimate principle of the world is not located in the Chaos or the Ocean or in the night, but in the One (*arché*) which is, precisely for Thales, water, the thing from which the world was formed.

In fact, in ancient Egypt, this inorganic but primordial *Noun* already prefigured the universe by its dimensions. The cosmos is at the level of the demiurge itself: "The Noun which carried Atoum and whose dimension is that of the sky and whose width is that of the earth" (*The Sarcophagus Texts*, 78 B1C).

Thus the sun (*Râ*) rose out of the liquid magma of his own will with a luminous spark. "I am the Eternal, I am Ra who came out of Noun... I am the master of light" (*Book of the Dead*, chapter 153 B).

We therefore have the following schema: *Noun (Nounou)*, fluid, liquid ether; Ra arises from the *Noun* (Atoum or Ra, or Atoum-Ra, the ancient sun-god of the city of Heliopolis, plunged in the primordial liquid with the potential existence of the gods). On the first day, Atoum, out of the *Noun*, brings forth the twin divinities: God *Shou* and Goddess *Tefnut*, the first couple created. The air and humidity necessary to life had thus taken form at the same time the temporal dimensions of the potential universe were given. "Shou is eternal time and Tefnut infinite time" (*The Sarcophagus Texts*, 80 B1C). Shou is eternity and Tefnut immensity. Shou and Tefnut then gave birth to the spatial elements of the universe: *Geb*, God of the earth and *Nut*, Goddess of the sky. In Egyptian thought the earth is the male element, the sky the female; the sky being the fertile principle of the world by the fact that it conceals the life-giving light. *Geb* and *Nut* had four children: *Osiris*, symbol of the fertile powers of the soil, and *Isis*, the equilibrium of life; *Seth*, symbol of sterility and of unhappy upheavals, and *Nephthys* who symbolises protection.

After the cosmic order, comes the terrestrial order. One can also recognise the moral antinomy between Good and Evil. The Ennead is perfect: Atoum emerged of the *Noun* , Shou and Tefnut, Geb and Nut, Osiris and Isis, Seth and Nephthys, created by Atoum.

Creation continues with that of humanity. The master of the universe created the four winds, the great flood, the inundation and each man resembling his neighbour (*The Sarcophagus Texts*, 1130).

This system, elaborated with great care, accounts for the genesis and the origins of the essential components of the universe:

(1) The initial principle, inexplicable: the *Noun*, foundation of the whole later universe.

(2) *Atoum-Râ*, the demiurge, emerges from the *Noun:* creative, luminous intelligence, springs from raw, unorganised, primordial matter.

(3) Advent of the cosmic order: *Atoum-Râ* creates *Shou* (air, atmosphere) and Tefnut (humidity), the

eternity and immensity of the universe.

(4) Advent of the terrestrial and celestial order: *Geb,* the earth, and *Nut,* the sky with the all-powerful sun.

(5) Advent of human order: *Osiris* and *Isis, Seth* and *Nephthys,* Good and Evil, the balance of sterility, the fertilising valley of the Nile and the arid desert.

These images, these speculations, born 4000 years before our era, in the consciousness of men and women of Pharaonic Egypt, lasted for nearly thirty centuries, justifying the sacred solar kingship of Egyptian sovereigns, supporting all the rituals, notably those linked to the beyond (solarisation of the deceased). The image of the rising and setting sun every day is an extraordinary psychological power in ancient Egypt: so life is a perpetual renewal of cosmic, divine and royal forces. Therefore the construction of obelisks, pyramids, temples, necropolises, palaces, always related to the all-powerful sun, invigorated and eternal.

(b) *The One and the Many*

There is a text which goes back to the fourth century before our era which expounds on how the existent came to exist: "The Master of the universe says: when I came to exist, then existence existed (*Kheper.i kheper kheperou*). I came to exist under the form of the Existent (*kheperou.kwi m kheperou nw kheperi*) who came into existence on the First Time (*kheper ms sp tpy*). Coming to exist under the mode of existence of the Existent, I therefore existed (*kheper.kwi m kheperou n kheperi kheper.i*). And so existence came to existence ((*kheper kheperou),* for I was anterior to the anterior gods whom I made, for I had anteriority upon these Anterior Gods, for my name was anterior to theirs (*pa ren .i),* for I made the anterior era as well as the Anterior Gods (*ntrw paoutiou)...* I therefore came to existence in the anterior era and a host of modes of existences came to existence from this beginning (*kheper âsha kheperou m tep-â)...* I did all that I did (*iri.n.i irryy nbt)* being alone (*wâi. kwi*)...I made the modes of existence from this force that is in me... And the modes of existence derived of the Existent were of multitudes (*âsha kheperou nw kheperi*)".

This text is complex by its form and its substance. The concept *kheper* constantly recurs: *kheper,* "to come into existence", "to exist", "to appear"; *kheper-djes-ef,* "the one who came to existence by himself"; *kheperou,* deriving from *kheper,* meaning: "form, configuration, modes of being, the forms, existence, modes of existence"; *kheper kheperou,* "existence came to existence", "existence existed", "existence came to be effective"; *kheperi, khepri,* "the Existent": the young Solar-God in the form of the sacred scarab.

As soon as he exists, the Existent brings existence into existence. This is immediate. A sort of sudden epiphany of the being in its very manifestation. For the Existent, to be is to exist effectively. It is of its own movement that the Existent comes to existence. He self-generated himself from himself. He is the absolute, perfect one.

From the Unicity will come the Multitude. Dialectics of the One and the Multiple: *wâi, One, âsha, Multitude.*

The modes of existence deriving from the Existent were multitudes. The Existent makes the other modes of existence by love (*merouty*). The Existent is the absolute being. He is also love and will. One must clearly emphasise that with the concept *kheper,* "to exist", "to become", the ancient Egyptians had some notions of the development of beings and things in the immense cosmic movement of the universe. This concept *kheper* is written with a hieroglyph which is a sacred scarab. This sacred Egyptian scarab is present elsewhere on the African continent, with the same symbolic value, in an identical cultural context: "A nicely carved box has a bulge in the shape of a scarab, the insect was created first and engendered the others... It is possible that there should be a connection between the importance given to the scarab as the one attributed to it by these people of Africa" (E. Torday and T.A. Joyce, *Notes ethnographiques,* op.cit., p.213). This concerns the scarab of the Kuba from central Zaire, very famous in the world for the fineness and greatness of their ancestral civilization.

The sacred scarab is the *One* who creates the *Multiple.* He is the first who engenders the others. The ancient Egyptians and the Kuba of Zaire gave to this insect the same importance to the development of the the world as to things. It is an encounter which could not be fortuitous, since these very Kuba of Zaire, as we saw it, present an identical schema of the world as the one of ancient Egypt.

For all that, all the African fauna from Pharaonic Egypt, receives a symbolic and metaphysical treatment: the lizard, the cobra, the falcon, the eagle, the leopard, the hippopotamus, the crocodile, the horned asp, the ibis, the owl, the bee, the bull, the monkey, the baboon, and other cercopitheci, etc., are animals which were and are still used as symbols for many African communities, since ancient Egypt.

Here is a cultural and psychological microstructure easily identifiable between the Egypto-Nubian Valley of the Nile and the rest of the African continent.

(c) *The knowledge of nature*

Any philosophy worthy of its name is always concerned with knowing physical nature scientifically. How was it in ancient Egypt?

Apart from its evident lyricism, the *Great Hymn to Aton* from King Akhenaton/Amenophis 1V (1372 - 1354 BC), denotes some scientific knowledge of nature.

1. The sun, origin of life on earth

The sun (*râ*) in its solar disc (*aton*), is the first to live (*shaâ*), and all the rest is born, lives, exists because of it: men, animals, vegetation, seasons, streams, mountains, work and days.

Although it is far (*wa.ti*), the sun nevertheless sends its rays onto the earth: "Your rays are on the earth" (*stwt.k hr to*). Indeed, the solar radiance is powerful, for it only takes a few moments to clear the huge distance between the earth and the sun. ("The sun is far, but it remains near": *wa.ti hn.ti*).

Akhenaton's hymn clearly says that the solar rays penetrate deeply in the sea (*stwt.k m-hnw W3d-Wr*). This is true: the solar atmosphere which sustains the crown, extends itself into space to millions of kilometres, reaching down to the depth of the ocean. Furthermore, this hymn tells us that the rays (*stwt*) emitted by the sun (*Râ*) reach our face (*tw.k m hr.sn*). But the trajectory of these rays (*šmt.k*, "your step, your coming") is not visible (*bw nw*). Indeed, all the radiations emitted by the sun are not visible, for instance, ultra-violet radiations are invisible to the naked human eye.

We can also read this: "You create millions of shapes from yourself" (*im.k*), but we cannot see them all, "for they remain hidden to the eye" (*iw št3 m hr p3*). It is true indeed, beings visible and invisible, are always creatures of the sun, so great is its creative power. A contemporary physicist, confirming the Egyptian vision, wrote: 'The visible world is the invisible organization of energy' (Heinz Pagels, *L'Univers Quantique*, translated from English by Jacques Corday, Paris, Inter-Editions, 1985, pp.342-343).

2. The green of the plants is due to solar energy

The plants, trees (*šnw, shenou*), the grass (*smw, semou*), "grow green" (*3h3h, akhakh,*) because of the sun's energy. This is true. Indeed, the green pigment of vegetation, chlorophyll, is only formed by light. So this energy of solar origin is introduced through photosynthesis in the great biochemical cycles of the globe. It may be conjectured here that the action of chlorophyllian vegetation was not known by the ancients as such, but it is really quite remarkable that Akhenaton's text should clearly attribute the green of the plant directly to sunlight.

3. The embryonic development of being

For Aristotle, the fact that an egg, so little organised in appearance, should develop into an adult, with a complex organization, was very mysterious.

The *Great Hymn to Aton* puts this fundamental question of the very reproduction of the species according to the method of descriptive embryology. Here is the text: "You make the seed develop in women. And create the semen of men. You vivify the son in the bosom of his mother". So the fact of reproduction is when the male puts the semen (*mw, mou,* "virile semen") in the woman's body where the eggs, the seeds (*m3yw, maiou*) exist, which are then fertilised and developed (*sekheper,* "to develop"; causative of *kheper,* "to become"). The fact is also that "semen and seeds", "spermatozoon and ovules", are creatures and fabrications of the solar energy in man and woman.

The embryonic development (*sekheper,* "the becomingness") is clearly stated by the Egyptian text: the developing organism is followed from the fertilised egg to the realization of a form capable of an autonomous and active life: "You vivify the son in the bosom of the mother". When the child is born, "You appease him with what dries his tears".

One sees that the *Great Hymn to Aton* deserves to be read otherwise than a text of monotheist profession of faith. This hymn also shows an exact knowledge of nature. In any case, the intuitions of this text are surprisingly scientifically precise when compared to modern scientific knowledge.

4. Philosophy as a reflection on science: its object and its method

Mathematics are generally considered as a rigorous science par excellence, whose object is studying the properties of beings (numbers, geometrical figures, etc.) through the methods or means of deductive reasoning. Mathematics also study the relations established between these entities.

Precisely in their conception of mathematics, the Egyptians truly defined both the object and the method of mathematics.

Let us now read the relevant text which is the very title of a book copied by the mathematician Ahmes from an ancient text around 1650 BC:

'Correct method for investigating nature, for knowing all that exists, every mystery, all secrets' (author's translation).

'Rules for enquiring into nature, and for knowing all that exists, (every) mystery, every secret' (translated by T. Eric Peet, 1923).

Peet's translation is rather loose and imprecise. We can compare it with the following technical vocabulary:

∗ *tp-hsb, tep-heseb*, "correct method", "accurate method"

∗*h3t, hat*, "descent", *m*, "in"; "study, research", "investigation": the human spirit must walk (hence the determinative of the step) to scrutinise the real; he must get down to (*m*) the facts, to examine them minutely and totally.

∗ *ht, khet*, "thing"; *khet nebet*, "all things". It refers to the whole of natural, objective facts; hence of nature itself, of concrete reality, of reality sensitive to the world.

﹡ *rh, rekh,* "to know", "to understand","to learn".

﹡ *ntt nbt, netet nebet,* "all that is", "all that exists": it is all real, the totality of what is, the world, nature, the universe with all its curiosities, all its wonders, all its enigmas.

﹡ *snkt, seneket,* "obscurity", "mystery";

﹡ *št3t, shetat,* "secret", (name); *št3, sheta,* "mysterious", "secret", "hidden", "difficult"; *št3w, shetaou,* "secrets", "mysteries", (religious).

So for the ancient Egyptians, mathematics (*rht, rekhet,* "number", "mathematics") deal with studying the entirety of nature, concrete reality as well as the enigmas and mysteries of the universe. It is a reflexive effort, a scientific investigation. So thanks to reason (*rh, rekh,* "to know", "knowledge", "reason"), the man who applies mathematics to scientific research in nature, can consequently succeed in smoothing the difficulties, the mysteries, the obscurities, the unknown.

The sensitive reality of the world, the enigmas of the universe, the mysteries, all these can be studied by man, according to a direct method, exact, rigorous, which can only be the mathematical method. All must be invested by mathematical research. The light of intelligence must remove all the difficulties, thanks to mathematics, thanks to the power of the number. Thanks to the science (*rh, rekh*) of the number (*rht, rekhet*), man can succeed in unveiling all of nature's secrets (*st3t nbt, shetat nebet*).

To sum up, the masterful thought contained in the *Rhind Mathematical Papyrus* is that mathematical science must be engaged in the methodical, operational control of the surrounding physical medium, while retaining a technical approach to explaining things.

The method (*tp-hsb, tep-heseb*) matters very much. It imposes rules (*tp-hsb, tep-heseb*), which, all together, represent rules or methods (*tp-hsb, tep-heseb*) to know (*rh, rekh*) nature (*ht, khet*), in all its aspects and its visible, invisible and hidden (*št3, sheta*) phenomena. This shows a highly scientific spirit when one follows an exact method to investigate nature (*n h3t m ht, en khat em khet*).

The method postulated here is in an authentic Egyptian text as an essential element of research, of knowledge, of science. So this text clearly stresses that method is required in scientific activity, and this rigorous method par excellence can only be mathematics.

There is no doubt that by going further, beyond the direct perception of plurality, *The Rhind Papyrus* already clearly reveals a perception of the logical aspect of numbers. Indeed, with a method one parts more and more with common, vulgar opinion.

In the whole of mediterranean antiquity, the ancient Egyptians were the first to praise the scientific ideal of mathematics. Pythagoras (6th century BC), who spent a long time studying in Egypt, directly owes to Egypt his mathematical philosophy, where number is considered as the matter and the form of the universe. Diophantes of Alexandria (c.325 - 410) reaffirms this Egyptian ideal of mathematics in the dedication to Dionysius, bishop of Alexandria, in his *Arithmetic,* 'started with an explanation of nature and the power of numbers...'

Conclusion

We could talk about African philosophy of the Pharaonic period for ages, but space does not permit. During the course of this essay, we have only highlighted a few concepts and themes of ancient Egyptian philosophy. We did not mention the notion of *Maât,* which sums up the moral code of ancient Egypt. The Egyptians of antiquity also discoursed at length on time, immortality and eternity. The power of the creative word appears for the first time, very explicitly, in ancient Egypt. We know that Plato, the Greek philosopher of eternal, unalterable ideas and of the Good Sovereign, praised Egyptian pedagogy and especially the arts: music, dance, painting, sculpture, because of their sacred character and their immemorial, temporal dimension. It is worth remembering, as an introduction to the questions that will be posed, that we have raised the following points:

1. The matter of "African philosophy", the cultural and historical context of such a question which still feeds so many unnecessary academic polemics.

2. African philosophy during the Pharaonic period, by drafting a methodology and by stating the documentation, for it is necessary to require a minimum of technical knowledge when one speaks of African philosophy of Pharaonic times.

3. A few concepts and themes of Egyptian philosophy: the notion of the uncreated (*Noun*), from which the world will take shape through the creative action of the Demiurge (*Râ, Atoum-Râ*); the dialectics of the *One* and the *Many* when we saw how the Existent came to existence, and how existence existed by the fact of coming to existence of the Existent; the knowledge of nature with the reading of the *Great Hymn to Aton* of King Akhenaton; the Egyptian reflection regarding mathematics, which are considered the most appropriate to know nature and all its mysteries.

Appendix: Questions

1. What does one understand by "philosophy?" Why has the existence of African philosophy been doubted for such a long time? What methodology can be envisaged for the study of African philosophy?

2. Can the history of African philosophy be outlined from antiquity up to the present? Which are the great chronological stages of such a history of philosophy for the whole African continent?

3. Briefly indicate the documentation on African

philosophy of the Pharaonic period, from the Old Kingdom (2815 - 2400 BC) up to the Late Period (1000 - 332 BC).

4. Anthologies of translated Egyptian texts exist, which anthologies do you know?

5. Present some major concepts and themes of Egyptian philosophy.

6. The *Great Hymn to Aton* by King Akhenaton (Amenophis IV, 1372 - 1354 BC) denotes great scientific knowledge of nature. Comment.

7. What is the Egyptian ideal of mathematics according to the title of the *Rhind Papyrus* (around 1650 BC)?

2.

THE AFRICAN ORIGIN OF PHILOSOPHY

I. **Etymology of the Word** *Philosophy*

E tymology is the science that studies the origin of words. What then is the origin of the word "philosophy?" It is very possible that the signification of the word philosophy should have the same origin as the word itself. It is therefore necessary to correctly answer this question.

In the Western world, the USA included, the agreed teaching of philosophy has this table of commandments:

1. Philosophy is of Greek essence — archaic Greece is therefore designated by Western nations as the birthplace of philosophy. The word in Greek, is

philosophy. The Greek language is the philosophy language *par excellence.*

2. Philosophy has nourished science. It preceded the sciences.   Science (physics, chemistry, mathematics, politics, aesthetics, logic, biology, sociology, etc.), was born of philosophy.

3. Philosophy is one of the privileged fields, where historical Western societies elaborate their destiny, their future.

4. Consequently, anywhere else in the world, in Precolombian America, Black Africa, Oceania, Asia (India, China, etc.), one will find thoughts, religions, cosmogonies, but never real philosophical systems: the thought or spirit of India, Chinese thought, the great Oriental monotheistic religions, the Black African myths, the Precolombian cosmogonies, etc.

5. So, only the Greeks founded universal reason, philosophy and science, in discovering rational existence, in inventing humanism, in constantly extending their analysis of the world.

These five dogmas or academic commandments, led the African intellectual elite, formed in Europe and the USA, to anxiously ask themselves this serious question: "Can one speak of African philosophy without misusing the term?" The answer is obviously, in the main, negative, until now. And a term was promptly invented for Black Africa: "ethno-philosophy", that is to say, something that resembles Greek philosophy but which cannot be philosophy, for, "objectively", philosophy can only be of Greek origin.

Isn't it then presumptuous, indeed senseless, to talk of the African origin of philosophy? How can Africa be designated, objectively, as the birthplace of Greek philosophy, and thus of the West, from Thales to Nietzsche and Heidegger, including Plato, Aristotle, Saint Thomas Aquinas, Descartes, Kant, Hegel?

This is a key question which can only be explicated in the light of linguistic facts and historical testimonies, verifiable by any competent researcher.

The compound word "philosophy" does not have an etymology, neither in Indo-European nor in Greek. This is obvious in the light of etymological science. We have *phílos,* adjective, which means: "loved, cherished, dear", in the passive, and "loving, benevolent" in the active, less common. The substantive *phílos,* means "friend". Adjective or substantive, the etymology of the word *phílos,* is unknown. There is nothing comparable to *phil* or *phílo* in other Indo-European languages. In other words, *phílos* cannot be explained in Greek, and it is not a word of Greek origin.

Let us now go to the second element of the compound word *philosophy.* We have *sophós,* "who knows, who dominates an art or a technique" and also; "learned, intelligent". The derivative *sophía,* Ionic *sophíē,* the first example of which can be found in Homer (*The Iliad,* 15, 412), means: "ability to do"; *sophía,* "the ability to do", can refer to a poet or a scientist, to practical knowledge and wisdom in general.

We have the following progressive compound of dependence: *phílo* "who love", *tó sophón,* "science, wisdom", hence *philosophía,* "liking for science, wisdom".

Philosophía can be applied to the liking of research, of science, of eloquence. The origins of the history of the words *sophós, sophía,* show how the Greeks went from a practical knowledge to a general (philosophical) knowledge. In modern Greek, we have *sophós*, "scientist", "scholar", and *sophía,* "knowledge", "wisdom". Yet the word *sophós* does not have an etymology, either in Indo-European or in Greek. No specialist could demonstrate otherwise.

So, the word "*philosophy*" does not have an etymology in Greek for either part: *philó* and *sophós.* This Greek word is not of Greek origin. The word philosophy, *philosophia, filosofia,* is not originally a Greek word. If, for the Western world, ancient Greece is the birthplace of *philosophy,* the word *philosophy* itself has no origin in Greek. And probably at the beginning , *philosophy* itself was foreign to Greece.

All these philosophical and etymological constructs are rigorously exact. The word *sophós* has no etymology in Greek. The etymology of *philos* is equally unknown in Greek. How can *philosophy* be of Greek essence or origin if the word *philosophy* itself is not a Greek word?

The Greek language, of Indo-European origin, has borrowed massively from other languages, notably from Semitic and Egyptian languages. This is the case, for instance, of the word we are interested in, *sophós,* "who knows, who masters an art or a technique", "learned, intelligent"; *tó sophón,* "science, wisdom"; *sophía,* "ability to do", "practical knowledge" and "wisdom, in general".

The Egyptian etymology of *sophós (sophón, sophía, sophíē)* is not so unbelievable, if we take into account the history of philosophy, which the Greeks received from the Egyptians. In fact, Isocrates (436 - 338 BC), designated Egypt as the cradle of *médicine*, for the well-being of the body, and of *philosophy* for the well-being of the soul: 'For the souls they (the Egyptian priests) revealed the practice of philosophy (*tāis dè psychāis philosophías askēsin katédeiksan*) which can, at the same time, set some rules and looked for the nature of things (*hē kaí nomothēsai kaì tēn physin tōn óntōn zētēsaii dúnatai* (Isocrates, *Busiris,* X1, 22).

From Egypt, philosophy reached Greece, with the Greeks being students of Egyptian priests. Among these Greek students, Isocrates expressly names Pythagoras of Samos, Greek philosopher and mathematician of the sixth century BC: 'He came to Egypt, and became the disciple (*mathētēs)* of the people there; he was the first to bring philosophy to Greece (*tēn t'állen philosophían prōtos eis toùs Héllēnas ekómisen)*' (Isocrates, ibid., X1, 28).

For Aristotle (384-322 BC), Egypt is the cradle of mathematics: 'So the mathematical arts (*mathēmatikaì téchnai*) were first (*prōton*, "at the beginning"), formed, constituted (*sun-ístēm* : Aristotle uses here the past tense which obviously indicated *anteriority*) only in Egypt (*perí Aígupton*)' (Aristotle, *Métaphysics*, A, 1, 981 b 23).

For the Greeks of antiquity, the "mathematical arts" included the following fields: geometry, the science of numbers (arithmetic), and astronomy. The Greeks only started to possess this scientific knowledge in the

days of Thales (end of seventh century to beginning
of sixth century BC). To be precise, Thales, Greek
mathematician and philosopher, founder of the first
Greek philosophical school in Miletus, Ionian city of
Asia Minor, was the first to use the word "wise" when
Damasias was archon of Athens (582 BC): 'He was
the first to be called *wise*' (*oũtos prõtos
ōnomasthe sophós,* Diogenes Laërtius).

Yet this Thales, founder of *sophía* (wisdom) in the
cultural and scientific history of the whole of Europe,
only had Egyptian priests for masters. 'He was taught
in Egypt under the direction of priests' (*epaideùthē
en Aiguptõ hupo tōn hiereōn*). So the first (*protos*)
representative of science, of wisdom, of philosophy,
in Greece, is an ex-pupil of the Egyptians. He is
Thales of Miletus.

For Isocrates, Egypt is the cradle of philosophy, that
is to say, the research of the nature of things (*tèn
physin tōn óntōn*). Also, for Aristotle, Egypt is the
cradle of "mathematical arts" (*mathēmatikaí
téchnai*), that is, arithmetic (*arithmētikē,* the theory of
numbers), the art of calculus, (*logistikē,* again,
arithmetic), geometry (*geometría*), that is, measuring
land, measuring areas and volumes, and finally,
astronomy (*astronomía*).

Egypt taught all these sciences, all these
techniques, all these arts to the Greeks, starting from
the first among them, Thales. We therefore have: *sb3,
seba,* "to instruct, to educate, to learn" in Pharaonic
Egyptian, in the *Pyramid Texts* (12, 9, etc.). The
derivative word *sb3wt.t, sebaou.t.,* means "teaching",
in both pharaonic and demotic (715 BC - 470 BC).
Coptic is *sbō,* in Sahadic and Boharic there is the
meaning of "teaching, education, intelligence". In

Coptic still, we have: *sabĕ, sabē,* "wise, intelligent, sensible, instructed".

Taking into account all that precedes (Egypt, cradle of medicine, of research into the nature of things, of wisdom, of mathematics), it is not so incredible that the Greek word *sophós,* which originally is neither Indo-European nor Greek, should derive from the Egyptian *sb3, seba, sbō, sabĕ*: sometimes the Egyptian /*b*/ is translated /*ph*/ in Greek. Example: *Nbt-Hwt* ,"house wife", Demotic *Nbt-Ht,* Coptic *Nebthō,* Greek *Nephtys;* the goddess *Nephtys,* sister of Isis.

In Greek, the Egyptian /*p* / is also often treated as /*ph(f)/: ip.t,* "a fruit measure", Demotic *ipy.t,* Coptic *oepiĕ, oipi,* "bushel", Hebrew *3ēfā* (Amos 8, 5), Greek *oiphi* (LXX), another measure. We also have: *k3p, kap,* "to burn" (incense), "to incense" (the gods), from the *Pyramids Texts (Pyr.* 1017, *Pyr.* 1718), which in Greek becomes *kyphi,* aromatic preparation used for religious rites (Plutarch, *Isis and Osiris,* 95, etc.).

The Egyptian /*f* / often becomes /*ph(f)/* in Greek: *sf.t,* "sword, knife"; Demotic *sfy, zfy,* "sword, knife"; Coptic *sēfē, sĕfi,* "sword, knife"; Mycenian *qi-is-pe-e* (from a tablet in Pylos) Homeric Greek *ksiphos,* "double-edged sword".

So, Egyptian bilabial /*p*/, /*b*/, /*f* /, very often correspond to the Greek phoneme /*ph (f)/*:

1. *sbō, sabĕ,* "learned" / *sophós,* "learned" (*s-b-/s-ph(f*)).

2. *Nbt-ht, Nebtho* / *Nephtys,* the goddess *Nephtys* (*n-b-th/n- ph(-f- th*)

3. *ip.t, oipi,* "measure"/*oiphi,* also a measure (*-p-/ph(f)-*)

4. *sf.t, sĕfe, sĕfi,* "sword" / *ksíphos,* "sword" (*s-f.ks-ph(f*).

The Greeks (Thales, Pythagoras, Plato, etc.) were taught, instructed and educated by Egyptian priests; the Egyptian *sbō*, "instructed" became *sophós* in Greek, with the derivative *sophía,* and the compound *sophón,* hence *philosophía.*

II. Definition of the Sage, of the Philosopher in Egypt, 2000 Years Before the Birth of the First Greek Philosopher

The philosopher is the friend of wisdom. He is instructed, and learns by studying nature. Philosophy is therefore the exercise of reason in the fields of thought and action. The result of this is a conception of the problems of life, of the world. Often, the conduct of the philosopher is reflective and moderate, prudent, circumspect and reserved. He acts with wisdom. The kings Antef and Mentuhotep form the eleventh dynasty from 2052 BC. A decisive text from Antef clearly defines the sage, the philosopher, according to the canons of the ancient Egyptians.

Here is the text, translated by the German Egyptologist Hellmut Brunner: '(He is the one) whose heart is informed about these things which would be otherwise ignored, the one who is clear-sighted when he is deep into a problem, the one who is moderate in his actions, who penetrates ancient writings, whose advice is (sought) to unravel complications, who is really wise, who instructed his own heart, who stays awake at night as he looks for the right paths, who surpasses what he accomplished yesterday, who is wiser than a sage, who brought himself to wisdom, who asks for advice and sees to it that he is asked advice' (*Inscription of Antef,* 12th dynasty: Middle Empire, 11th and 12th dynasties, 2052 - 1778 BC).

So the Egyptian sage should be informed of all these things, clear sighted in the examination of a problem, moderate in action. He had to know the tradition in studying ancient texts. He surely had some experience of human existence in order to unravel all these complicated questions. He had to apply himself to thought, meditation, day and night, in order to find the "correct paths". Constantly dissatisfied, he is always in search of the better and the best. A sage sees to it that he is asked for advice, while he himself asks for advice.

This is the lively, impressive portrait of the philosopher in ancient Egypt. Such a sage owed it to himself to know the cause of all things, natural, social and human. To be a philosopher in Pharaonic times, one had to be a sage and a scientist at the same time.

There are no similar or comparable texts, around 2052 BC, in the ancient Mediterranean and Mesopotamian world, which give you such an ample definition of the sage, the philosopher, the friend of wisdom, with such clarity and exactitude. Isocrates (436 - 338 BC) is therefore quite right to consider Egypt as the cradle, the birthplace of philosophy, in the proper sense of the term.

In the Egyptian language we have:

s3i, sai, Coptic *sŏi,*   "to be wise, prudent"; "to be satisfied"

(*The Pyramid Texts,* 551, etc.)

s3.t, sa.t,   "prudence, wisdom" (Sinouché, B 48)
s33, saa,   "wise man".

Wisdom in ancient Egypt is linked to reason, knowledge, action, prudence, morality. The sage is eternally dissatisfied, for he must constantly better himself, in wisdom, in his meditation, his action, his conduct.

The authentic sage, for the ancient Egyptians, must have shown a strong inclination for erudition, to have had faith in the organising virtues of the intellect, pursued essential qualities. He was a sort of "universal technician", dedicated to rational, human culture, having a mind constantly awake before things and men.

Indeed, the ancient Egyptians left pyramids, obelisks, temples, stelae, but one often forgets the huge philosophical work accomplished by them, during almost thirty centuries. But the Greeks had tasted the intellectual elegance and depth of the ancient Egyptians and hungered for more. In the eye of the history of philosophy in the world, we have the following chronology:

✳ 2052 - 1778 BC in the Middle Empire, an *Inscription of King Antef* defines the sage, the philosopher. It is the first attempt to define the philosopher in the cultural and scientific history of mankind;

✳ c. 1400 and 2000 BC, the composition of the Veda, "knowledge, understanding", the sacred writing of Hinduism (*Rig-Veda, Sama-Veda, Yajur-Veda, Atharva-Veda*);

✳ c. 800 BC the *Upanishad,* the Sanskrit texts of a philosophical — religious nature;

✳ end of 7th - beginning of 6th century BC: Thales,

born in Miletus (Asia Minor), founder of the Ionian School, which starts philosophical thought in Greece; the Seven Sages in Greece (6th century);

* c. 570 BC: *Kungfuzi* (Kung fu tsi, Confucius), Chinese philosopher and statesman;

* c.500 BC: *Laozi* (Lao-tse, Lao-tseu) whose teachings are presented in the *Daodejing* (Tao-tö King);

* c.560 - 480 BC: *Buddha* ("the sage", "the" enlightened"), Siddharta Gautama, founder of Bhuddism;

* 600 BC: *Pythagoras*, Greek philosopher and mathematician, born in Samos, a Greek island in the Aegean sea;

* 470 - 399 BC: *Socrates*

* 427 - 347 BC *Plato:* disciple of Socrates;

* 384 - 322 BC: *Aristotle,* tutor of Alexander of Macedonia, founder of the peripatetic school;

* c.600 - 900 AD, classical apogee of the Mayan civilization: *Popol-Vuh.*

At this point, one can objectively affirm, following Isocrates of Athens (436 - 338 BC), that Egypt is the cradle of philosophy: the first broad and complete definition of the "sage" is Egyptian. The Greek word *"sophós"*, "instructed", is not etymologically explainable in Indo-European or even in Greek. It is probably derived from the Egyptian *sbo,* "instructed, wise". Consequently, it is quite exact in the eye of the history of philosophy to say that philosophy is of African origin, since the first definition of "the sage, the philosopher", in the history of mankind, is to be found in Africa, precisely in Egypt.

There is obviously more, for instance, the training of the first Greek philosophers by Egyptian priests. In this sense too, one can talk about the *African origin of Greek philosophy.*

III. **Egypt Contributed to the Birth of Greek Philosophy**

We do not know any Greek philosophers at the time of the development of the Mycenian civilization, around 1600 BC. Even less during the Dorian invasions, around 1200 BC. The Minoan writing called *Linear B* in Crete, around 1500 BC, did not reveal any philosophical or scientific texts. The Greeks adopted Phoenician writing around 800 BC, and completed it by adding signs, which represented vowels. So before their expansion towards the East and Egypt, the Greeks did not know anything about science or philosophy. Historically, Greece only awoke to science and philosophy *after* the sixth century BC. This is a well established, unarguable historical fact.

Geographically, Greek philosophy was born in Asia Minor, in the towns of Miletus, Colophon, Clazomenae, Epheseus, Cnidus, respectively the hometowns of Thales, Anaximander and Anaximenes, Xenophanes, Anaxagoras, Heraclites, and Eudoxus. Asia Minor is the name which the Greek and the Latin gave to the western part of Asia, south of the Black Sea. It is well and truly the Greece of Asia, this fringe of islands (Cos, Samos, Chios, Lesbos, etc.), and of the countries of Greek cities in antiquity, on the oriental west of the Aegean sea (Cnidus, Halicarnassus, Miletus, Ephesus, Colophon, Clazomenae, Mytilene, Pergamum, Cyzicus, etc.), which geographically is the immediate cradle of

Greek philosophy and sciences.

In antiquity the Greek scholars themselves would not dare talk about "a Greek miracle" because for them, philosophy was first born abroad: in Persia, Chaldea, India, and Egypt.   No Greek scholar affirmed otherwise.

Regarding the relations between Greece and Egypt, in the crucial matter of philosophy and science (geometry, mathematics, astronomy and medicine), the enlightening role of the Nile Valley was, for centuries, very preponderant, on the learned Greeks:

1. *Thales of Miletus*, mathematician and philosopher, born in Miletus (end of seventh, beginning of sixth century BC), founder of the Ionian school, studied under the direction of priests (*hupo tōn hieréōn*), his only masters in life.

2. *Solon of Athèns* (c. 640/558 BC), legislator, was a pupil of the old priest Sanchis, in Sais, ancient town of Lower Egypt, whose princes, governed Egypt from 663 to 525 BC.

3. *Pythagoras of Samos* (c.600 BC), philosopher, and mathematician, founder of the phythagorean school, spent almost twenty-two years studying in Egypt at Memphis and at Thebes, and above all with Egyptian priests.

4. *Xénophanes of Colophon*, (around the end of the sixth century), philosopher, founder of the eleatic school around 535 BC, went to Egypt where he exhorted the Egyptians not to honour so many

divinities. He also expressed his surprise at seeing the Egyptians beating their chests during public religious ceremonies, notably during festivals given in honour of Osiris.

5. *Anaxagoras of Clazomenae* (c. 500/428 BC), philosopher, he too went to Egypt in order to learn from Egyptian priests, a more exact science of nature.

6. *Pherecydes of Syros*, studied theology and science in Egypt.

7. *Empedocles of Acragas (Arigento* in Italian) (born just before 490 - died 438 BC), philosopher and legislator, developed the theory of opposites, being inspired by, according to Plutarch, the well-known myth of Osiris and Seth.

8. *Democritus of Abdera* (c.460 - 370 BC), philosopher, spent five years in Egypt (Diodorus Siculus, I, 98, 3) to learn geometry and astronomy: his master in Memphis was the priest Pamménès. According to the details of Democritus' work, established by the grammarian Thrasyllus (not the Greek naval commander, ed) who lived at the court of Tiberius (42 BC - 37 AD), Democritus would have written a book *On the hieroglyphs of Meroe.*

9. *Socrates* (c. 470 - 399 BC), philosopher, said to Phaedrus that the truth (*tò alethès*) is known by the ancients *(tōn protéron)*, that the Egyptian god Thoth was the first *(prōton)* to discover the science of numbers (*arithmón*), calculus (*logismòn*), geometry (*geōmetrían*), astronomy (*astronomían*), and even backgammon (*petteías*) and dices (*kubéias*), and

lastly, and above all, writing (*grámmata*): (Plato, *Phaedrus,* 274 c-d).

10. *Plato of Athens* (427 - 347 BC), philosopher, studied in Egypt, in Memphis exactly, with the priest Khnouphis and at Heliopolis with the priest SeKnouphis:

  * Birth of Plato in Athens: 7th May, 427;

  * at the age of twenty, in 407, Plato was a disciple of Socrates;

  * at twenty-eight, in 399, after Socrates' death (c. 470 - 399 BC), Plato travels to complete his studies in Megara where Euclid of Megara (450 - 380 BC) was teaching; Megara — Greek city on the isthmus of Corinthia, prosperous in the seventh and sixth centuries BC; in Cyrene, ancient city of North Africa, founded by the Dorians in 630 BC, capital of Cyrenaic (north-east region of Libya) under the mathematician Theodorus; in Crotona in Italy, under Philolaos, famous pythagorean who lived around 470 BC; finally, in Egypt, at Memphis and at Heliopolis;

  * in 387 BC Plato returned to Athens and founded the Academy at the age of forty, after twelve years of travel and study. This philosophical school, founded by Plato in the neighbouring gardens of Athens, lasted from the fourth to the first centuries BC.

Of all the dialogues of Plato, twenty-eight have survived. In almost twelve dialogues, Plato mentions Egypt abundantly in varied ways. The proportion is enormous: forty-two per cent of Plato's total known work.

Indeed, Plato talks about Egypt in these works written between 390/385: *Gorgias, Euthdèmus, Menexenus,* in the work written between 385/370:

Phaedo, Republic, Phaedrus; and in the works written between 370/347 BC: *Politics, Timaeus* and *Critias, Philebus, Laws.* Even in *Epinomis*, Egypt is mentioned.

11. Aristotle (384 - 322 BC), born in Stariga (Stavros), ancient city of Macedonia, the historical region of the Balkans peninsula, shared today between Bulgaria, Greece and Yugoslavia, is the founder of the peripatetic school, and tutor of Alexander of Macedonia (356 - 323 BC), conqueror of Egypt and the Orient, King of Macedonia from 336 - 323 BC.

It seems that Aristotle visited Egypt, according to a technical passage from the *Meteorologicals* (352 b 20) where it is a question of an explanation for the emergence of the delta of the Nile: the Egyptians' country is manifestly the work of the river, 'This is clear (*kaì toûto dēlón esti*) to one who sees *(horônti)* as he descends along *(katá)* this country *(tèn chóran autèn)*'.

The verb *horáō* employed by Aristotle, is a verb of *perception.* It means: "to see, to perceive with the sight organ". In its absolute sense, this verb means "to have the use of sight". This verb *horáō* is very concrete. Hence its other meanings: "to look", "to visit someone". The preposition *katá*, constructed here with the accusative, concerns space and means: "descending along". To the one who can see, that is, who can examine with attention, descending the Valley of the Nile from the Delta towards Upper Egypt (*dēlón esti*), it is clear that the Egyptian country is well and truly the work of the Nile. This is what Aristotle says, using precise, concrete Greek terms, using beautiful syntax. The conclusion is that Aristotle truly saw for himself the work of the Nile in the making of the fertile strip of the Nile Valley.

Today, contemporary science agrees with Aristotle regarding the problem of the emergence of the Delta:

1. 3500 BC, from this moment, the level of the sea lowered under three metres, the highest parts of the future Delta of the Nile are yet to emerge.

2. 3000 BC, the whole present surface of the Delta progressively emerged out of water. This represents an average of more than 3500 new hectares emerging every year from the sea — thanks to the the silt brought down by the Nile for 5000 years, with each of its yearly floods; therefore in 3000 BC, half of the Delta had already emerged from the sea.

This Delta country is well and truly the work of the Nile. It is also obvious that the Egyptian civilization could not be born in the Delta. In other words, the kingdom of the South (Upper Egypt), precedes the kingdom of the North (Lower Egypt). After all, it is a king of the South, Menes (Narmer) who conquered the kingdom of the North, the Delta, constituting the union of the Double-Country, that is Upper and Lower Egypt.

For Aristotle (*Meteorologicals*, I, 14 352 b), the Egyptians were the most ancient of men (*archaiotatoi tōn anthrōpōn*), that is to say, that the Egyptians engaged, since time immemorial, on the paths of civilization, are thence the first creators of civilization, in particular mathematics and astronomy. This historically confirmed report, established by

Aristotle, was obviously unquestionable in his eyes.

. 12. *The Library of Alexandria*: The two libraries of the temple of Edfu (Horus' Temple) and of the Ramesseum in Thebes, served as models for Ptolemy Soter for the construction of the Library of Alexandria; and the School of Alexandria trained scientists in several fields of knowledge from 305 BC - 270 AD; therefore during the centuries of decadence in Greece: Euclid, the mathematician; Callimachus, the poet and grammarian; Manetho, Egyptian priest and historian, from the third century BC; Erasistratus, the physiologist; Herophilus, the anatomist; Erastothenes, mathematician, astronomer and philosopher (c. 284/275 - 195); Archimedes (287 - 212 BC);   Appollonius   of   Perga,   Hipparchus, Agatharchides, Sotion, Ctesibius, Hero, Sosigenes, Strabo, Claude, Ptolemy, Diophantes, Clement of Alexandria (c. 150-between 211 - 216), Ammonius Saccas (third century A. D). Origen (c.183/186 - 252/254), Longinus, Plotinus of Lycopolis, in Egypt (c.203/205 - 270), etc.

One therefore follows a huge and powerful civilizing current in the history of humanity: Pharaonic Egypt/Ancient Egypt, School of Alexandria, the Greco-Roman world, the Middle Ages, Western modern times.

In this long historical and cultural chain, Pharaonic Egypt is obviously the first link, and the School of Alexandria was truly the cultural and spiritual junction between East and West, long before the Arabs.

This huge, powerful, civilizing current, which goes from the banks of the Nile to those of the Tiber, is an historical fact, well established, but rarely taught: Rome was the heir of hellenistic Egypt, and thus of glorious pharaonic Egypt (Jean Leclant, *Meroe et Rome*, in "Studia Meroitica 1984", Meroitica, No. 10, 1989, pp.29-45; p.44 . These are the proceedings of the 5th Congrès International des Etudes Meroïtiques, Rome 1984: edited by Sergio Donadoni and Stefen Wenig, Akademie-Verlag, Berlin, 1989).

IV. Greeks in the Nile Valley: Itinerary and Cost of the Journey

Greeks from every where, Ionians, Carians of Asia Minor, from Cyrene, Greeks of the islands and the mainland, speak of the whole of Egypt, land of the old civilization and of a prodigious fertility under the Pharaohs of the twenty-fifth dynasty (664 - 525 BC): Psammeticus I, Necho II, Psammeticus II, Apries and Amasis, kings buried in the temple of Neith at Sais.

During this dynasty, Egypt experienced a wonderful political, intellectual, artistic and religious renaissance. The court and the administration were reconstituted after the expulsion of the Assyrians and the Ethiopians (Nubians) of the twenty-fifth dynasty; the Demotic writing appeared, all the big cities were distinguished by religious buildings.

Egypt then starts trading with the Greeks: Naucratis

on the canopic branch of the Nile, near Sais, was a Greek commercial trading post founded by the Milesians, under Psammeticus I (seventh century BC). Naucratis will only be outshined at the founding of Alexandria in 322 BC by Alexander of Macedonia.

King Amasis (not to be mistaken with the Greek potter Amasis, around 550 - 525 BC) was even more favourable to the Greeks, who established themselves everywhere: at Memphis, at Abydos, in the Great Oasis. Herodotus reports this: 'Friend of the Greeks, Amasis gave some of them tokens of his benevolence... Amasis concluded friendship and alliance with the Cyreneans... Amasis also consecrated offerings in Greek countries: in Cyrene, Lisbos, Samos, Hera... He was the first in the world (that is, the first Egyptian) to seize the island of Cyprus and forced it to pay tribute' (Herodotus, *The Histoires*, Book II, §§ 178, 181, 182).

Yet, in the Valley of the Nile, at this period, instruction was widespread in the country. Each big city had one or more schools which depended on temples, which were powerful and venerable, priestly, and hierarchical. Sais, Bubastis, Tanis, Heliopolis, Memphis, Hermopolis, Abydos and Thebes had great scientists who could not do without exploiting the ancient sacerdotal libraries, for example, the library of the Temple of Horus, at Edfu, the library of Tebtunis, at Fayum, including numerous literary texts, religious or scientific treaties; the private libraries of Thebes, the one in Deir el-Medina (the

Chester Beatty collection) which included magical texts, popular and mythological tales, psalms, literary and medical texts. The priestly colleges of Heliopolis had a universal reputation. Thebes of the hundred doors (Homer) was the most international town in Mediterranean antiquity. To travel to Egypt, the Greek traders, students, tourists, mercenaries, and adventurers, inevitably used one or the other of these routes:

1. *The Oriental route:* the harbour of Phalera in the sixth century; then, from Piraeus (port and suburb of Athens) in the fifth and fourth centuries. The Cyclades (Greek islands of the Aegean Sea, around Delos), the shores of Lycia (south-east of Asia Minor) and Pamphylia (southern country of Asia Minor, between Lycia and Cilicia); Cyprus (the copper island): this route was already frequented during Syrian-Mycenian times.

2. *The Western route :* it is the direct route between Greece and Egypt: this route was equally followed in Mycenian times (see *The Odyssey,* XLV, 252 -257).

The cost of the journey? Socrates reminds Callicles that the cost of the journey to Egypt is two drachmas on disembarking (Plato, *Gorgias,* 511 d: *apobibása eis tón liména dúo drachmàs. Gorgias* is a dialogue written by Plato between 390 and 385 BC).

The value of money varied from one city to another in ancient Greece, but the ones used in Egina, between Peloponnesia and Athens, which carried on the obverse side (of the coins), the head of Athena and on the reverse, the owl of the goddess, had an international value: these coins were made of silver. One drachma was worth six obolus, about 0.97 French francs or two drachmas were equivalent to one attic stature, about 1.94 French francs. When it comes to the weight, a drachma (6 obolus) weighed 4.32 grammes.

It is obvious that Socrates would have kept secret the price of the journey from Athens to Egypt if it did not correspond to reality. The Greeks who travelled to Egypt therefore paid for their crossing on disembarking in Egypt, at the end of the journey.

The relations between Greece and Egypt were not legendary, but real. On the contrary, they were easy and numerous, and lasted centuries. This finally created a high opinion of Egypt in the Greek collective mentality. But this Egyptian mirage which always haunted the Greek spirit, was justified by the fact that Egypt was the country of literature, art and philosophy, millennia before the birth of intellectual life in Greece.

And it is not surprising that Greece should owe to Egypt its first scientists and philosophers. Egyptian thought has formed the basis for Greek thought, just as today North American science and technology dominate and fascinate the entire world. It is simply a matter of the overwhelming superiority of the USA! In antiquity, during the period we are discussing, the scientific supremacy of Egypt had no equivalent in Greece. And the Greeks had no ethnic complex about going and learning in the Nile Valley, under the authority of the wise Egyptians.

Since this prestigious Egyptian civilization is owed to the Black Africans who then lived in the Nile Valley, responsible from start to finish for Pharaonic civilization, in the teaching of ancient history, of the history of ideas, modern Eurocentric scholars seem to ignore all these truths and to dismiss the testimonies of the Greeks themselves, not without historic falsification: 'The historical consciousness of mankind', stated Professor Cheikh Anta Diop, 'is still suffering from these voluntary distortions of history'. One must react against this here and now for a truthful presentation of the cultural evolution of humanity.

V. What the Greeks learnt in the Nile Valley

One must definitely abandon the preposterous idea, according to which Pharaonic Egypt, instead of "science", only knew "empirical recipes". Objectively, it is difficult to conceive that the Greeks who went to the Nile Valley to learn and satisfy their intellectual curiosity with Egyptian priests, should have done so only to be initiated to "empirical recipes". To think so, is to give proof of a great judgement of ignorance.

Actually, by going to the Nile Valley for their training, the Greeks were initiated into real scientific and philosophical knowledge:

1. Metaphysics, Philosophy

(a) The Egyptians were the first to state (*prōtoi*) the doctrine of the immortality of man's soul (*ōs anthrōpou psychē athánatós esti*), says Herodotus (II, 123). This is correct. From the earliest time of their history, the Egyptians had clearly stated that something of man, his "double" (*ka*), his "soul" (*ba*), survived the death of the body. This belief in immortality is typically Egyptian, well before the religion of the near East. The theme of the judgement of the dead is also Egyptian in origin.

(b) In referring to the origin of philosophy, Diogenes Laertius (third century AD), in his precious work, *Life, Doctrines and Maxims of Renowned Philosophers*, sums up Egyptian philosophy in the introduction: 'There is the first principle, matter; then the four elements dissociated; then living beings were formed. The sun and the moon are gods. One was called Osiris, the other was Isis... They thought that the world had had a beginning, that it would have an end, that it was spherical, that the stars were made of fire, and that their heat gave birth to everything on the surface of the earth; that the soul was eternal, that rain came from a transformation of air'. This is accurate. The Egyptian *Noun* is indeed the first principle of Egyptian philosophy and this first principle is matter, a liquid, fluid ether. The four elements: water, earth, fire, air, were identified by Egyptian priests who made them constituent elements in the advent and evolution of the universe, millennia before the birth of Thales, the founder of Greek philosophy. To imagine that the world should be spherical, that the stars should be made of fire, that the heat of the sun gave life to everything on earth, and that rain came from air, from the clouds, condensing the evaporated water (the air is the gas which forms the atmosphere, it contains vapour, etc.)... This is not ordinary and quite clearly separates itself from the non-scientific knowledge of then public opinion.

(c) The "mysteries" were an immense part of Egyptian knowledge: mystery of life and death, mystery of the power of the number, mystery of the beyond, mystery of the gods, mystery of the human spirit: 'Do not reveal the rituals that you see in every mystery in the temples' (Emil Chassinat, *Le Temple d'Edfou*, Cairo, IFAO, 1928, p.361, line 3). And it is accepted that the "taste for mystery" of Pythagoras and of pythagoreans comes directly from Egypt.

2. Astronomy

(a) *The obliqueness of the ecliptic on the equator:* 'Oenopides of Chios learned from the Egyptians the knowledge of the orbit of the sun which, because of its oblique course, moves in an opposite direction to the other stars' (Diodorus Siculus, *Bibliothèque Historique*, I, part two, XCVIII). Oenopides of Chios was a pythagorean. He was from Chios, a Greek island in the Aegean sea. This text, by Diodorus Siculus, a Greek historian born in Agyrion (first century B.C.) clearly affirms that Oenopides learned an important astronomical discovery from the Egyptians: the obliqueness of the ecliptic on the equator, that is to say, the angle of the plan of the ecliptic with the one of the celestial equator. The ecliptic is the great circle containing the centres of the earth and the sun which cuts the celestial sphere, in the case of Egyptian and Dogon astronomy. Indeed, the Dogon of Mali (West Africa) know how to determine, mathematically and graphically, the positions of the sun on the ecliptic (See Dominique Zahan, *"Etudes sur la cosmologie des Dogon et des Bambaras du Soudan Français. 1. - La notion d'écliptique chez les Dogons et les Bambaras,"* in *Africa* (London), Vol. XXI, January, 1951, No. 1, pp.13 -23).

(b) *Eclipses — comets*: Egyptian astronomy could 'observe with great exactitude the eclipses of the sun and the moon, and calculate them in advance, in order to predict in the greatest detail, and infallibly, these kinds of phenomena' (*Bibliothèque historique,* I, 50). This text, of exemplary precision, shows that the encounters of the sun and the moon were known to Egyptian scientists who could calculate them in advance. The astronomer-priests surely taught Thales (who predicted an eclipse of the sun in 585 BC) a method to calculate eclipses. Let us not forget that the most ancient Egyptian astronomical texts date back to the ninth dynasty (c.2150 BC). For instance, they gave the names of thirty-six stars which rise within ten days of each other, at the same time as the sun. Regarding comets, astronomers seem to have recorded, under Thutmosis III (1504 - 1450) the apparition of Halley's comet (Serge Sauneron, article in the *Dictionnaire de la civilisation Egyptienne*, Paris, 1959.) This is very possible, for if comets, visible to the naked eye, are rare, comets which describe elliptic orbits are periodically observable: this is the case of Halley's and Encke's comets.

(c) *The course of stars and planets*: the course of the stars and planets was also a preoccupation of the Egyptians. 'Four thousand years ago, the Egyptians knew that the earth moved in space and they did not fear to attribute the knowledge of this astronomical fact to the generations who had preceded them centuries ago' (F. Chabas, Egyptologist, "*Sur un texte égyptien relatif au mouvement de la terre*", in *Bibliothèque Egyptologique,* Paris, Ernest Leroux, 1903, Vol. XI, pp.1-3; p.12).

(d) *The origin of Lunar light*: a late Egyptian text can be read as follows, '(God-moon) Light of the night, image of Amon's left eye which rises East while Aton (the sun) is in the West. Thebes is inundated by its brilliance, for the left eye receives the light of the right eye...' This text is essential. The sun and the moon are defined like the two eyes of the sky. When the sun disappears to the eyes of the living, then the moon takes over, but the lunar light is owed to the right eye, that is, the sun. This is a scientific explanation of the lunar light.

(e) *The astronomical calendar*: In antiquity the Egyptian civil calendar was the only calendar to be based on astronomy; this Egyptian calendar is the very foundation of our present calendar. Callimachus, poet and grammarian of Alexandria, born in Cyrene (c. 310-235 BC), thinks that Thales was the first to make a calendar, and taught sailors to be led by the great Bear. This scientist from Alexandria simply forgets that Thales received his scientific education in Egypt, where the annual calendar of 365 days had been known as early as 4200 BC, and where the Great Bear, a constellation of the boreal hemisphere, was well and truly identified by the Egyptians, who called it *Meskhetyou.*

3 Medicine

(a) *The first treaty of cardiology*: *The Ebers Papyrus*, which dates from the ninth year of the reign of Amenophis I (1557 - 1530 BC) contains theoretical reflections on the problems of life and health. Paragraph 854a states the anatomy and physiology of the heart, showing precisely that the Egyptians had a clear notion of arterial vascularisation and of the whole circulatory system. Egyptian doctors could take the pulse in a precise and general manner. Cardiac pathology had also naturally attracted the attention of Egyptian doctors: paragraph 855 of the *Ebers Papyrus* notes the state of cardiac deficiency and its hepatic and pulmonary repercussions. The circulation of the blood from the heart to the periphery was known to the Egyptians.

(b) *The first treatise of general and osseous surgery of mankind*: it is the *Edwin Smith Papyrus*, which dates from the beginning of the eighth dynasty (1567 BC) — the *Book of Wounds* — contains the study of forty-eight surgical cases of wounds and lesions, from

head to toes, following a most rigorous method:
entitled examination or observation, diagnosis,
prognosis, treatment. The surgeons of ancient Egypt
were able to establish anatomical links between the
reach of the central system and the peripheral
reach, thence identifying the unit of innervation
(between the central and peripheral nerves).

(c) *The Egyptians practised dissection*: the
identification of the masseter muscle which starts from
the external angle of the lower jaw up to the
temporal bone, by Egyptian surgeons, is proof of the
practice of dissection.

(d) *The aphasices of comprehension and of
expression.* The aphasia of Wernicke, German
neurologist (1848 - 1905), and of Broca, French
surgeon and anthropologist (1848 - 1880), were
known to the ancient Egyptians: *Edwin Smith
Papyrus*, case 22.

(e) *Homer* (c. 850 BC) shamelessly praised Egypt as
the country 'where the doctors are the first scientists
of the world' (*The Odyssey*, IV, 231). The most learned
scientists in the world, in antiquity, (Mesopotamia,
Phoenicia, land of the Hittites, Greece, Persia, etc.),
were to be found in Egypt where Hippocrates (c. 460
- 377 BC) and Galieri (c.131 - 201) had consulted
Egyptian medical works in the temple of Imhotep in
Memphis.

4. Mathematics

(a) *Egyptian mathematics form a homogeneous, harmonious and complete whole*: in spite of its 'pragmatic empirical and concrete' applications, 'the pragmatic appearance of the Egyptian calculus reveals the properly intellectual competence of mathematical thought'... (*Les étapes de la philoso-sophie mathématique.* Paris, Presse Universitaire de France, 1947, p.32).

There are, therefore, arithmetical rules behind the calculation of the Egyptian mathematical papyrus: 'The operations are themselves similar because there are rules: the rules are co-ordinated because they are part of an organised and rational arithmetic. Whole numbers, even, odd, primary numbers, fractions of one, of two, of any number, proper and improper fractions, squares, powers, square roots, addition, subtraction, with a search for the complement, multiplication and division under multiple forms, proportions, progressions, etc... Everything is there and is treated in such a way that modern critics had nothing to add' (O. Gillain, *La science Egyptienne. L'Arithmétique au Moyen Empire,* Bruxelles, F.E.R.E., 1927, p.301).

Egyptians could calculate the surface of the square, the rectangle, the triangle, the trapezium, the circle, with a good approximation of *pi*, the semisphere. They could also precisely calculate the volume of the cube, the prism, the circular cylinder, the pyramid, the trunk (frustum) of the square-based pyramid.

Let us take an example, problem forty-one from the
Rhind Papyrus. It refers to the volume (*shaâ*) of a
circular cylinder (*deben*), diameter 9, height 10. The
deben, revolving cylinder or right circular cylinder, is
the shape created by the rotation of a rectangle
around one of its sides. The two circles created
are equal; these are the *bases* and their length is the
height of the cylinder. Therefore, the volume of a
cylinder is equal to the surface of the circle,
multiplied by the height. This is a formula applied by
the Egyptian scribe around 1650 BC, that is, ten
centuries before the birth of the first mathematician
of the Greek world, Thales (c. 640 - 546 BC).

Around 1850 BC, Egyptian mathematicians could
accurately calculate the volume of the trunk of a
truncated pyramid (problem 14 of the *Moscow
Papyrus*). The trunk of a pyramid is the portion of the
pyramid situated between the base and the section
through a parallel plan at the base. The *bases* of the
trunk, the great and little bases, are similar polygons.
The lateral sides are *trapeziums.* The distance
between the bases is the *height* of the trunk. When
the trunk of the pyramid is regular, that is, when it is
obtained by cutting a regular pyramid through a
plan parallel to its base, we obtain the following: its
bases are *regular polygons*; its lateral sides are *equal
isosceles trapeziums,* and the height of one of them is
the *apothermus* of the trunk. The volume of a
pyramid is equal to a third of the surface of the base
x the height. Therefore, *the volume of the trunk of a*

pyramid is equal to the sum of the volume of three pyramids, having in common the height of the trunk, and respectively the great base, the little base and the proportional middle one between the two bases.

There is no other formula to find accurately the volume of the trunk of a truncated pyramid. Indeed, the solution of the scribe is absolutely correct, faultless. In Egypt, the volume of the pyramid was mathematically calculated around 1850 BC, and in Greece, this kind of problem only appears with Euclid in his *Elements,* which comprises thirteen books (465 terms) which can be traced back to 300 BC (see Book XIII, construction of regular polyhedrons).

The calculation of the *seked,* the angle of inclination of a pyramid, corresponds to what we call today the cotangent; it is well and truly a trigonometric relation between the horizontal base of the pyramid and its height. To say that this is an "empirical", "approximate" calculation, etc., is proof of dishonesty.

(b) *There was plenty to teach the Greeks*: c. 1850 (the *Moscow Papyrus*) or c. 1650 (the *Rhind Papyrus*), that is, when the Egyptians are setting and solving difficult mathematical problems (surface of a semisphere, volume of a circular cylinder, volume of the trunk of a pyramid, calculation of the cotangent of the angle of the pyramid, etc.), there is, strictly speaking, nothing in Greece at this time concerning maths or sciences generally. Greek science was not born from thin air, not even from Greek myths, but well and truly from the knowledge gathered millennia earlier by the Babylonians and the Egyptians. This is the absolute historical truth.

For all that, Herodotus, Greek historian of Halicar-nassus (488 - 470 BC), traces the origin of Greek geometry back to Egypt (Herodotus, II, 109). For Aristotle (384 - 322 BC) Egypt was the cradle of "mathematical arts" (*Metaphysics*, A, 1, 981 b 23).

The only great *historical* text that we inherited from Greek antiquity, concerning the history of maths, is the *Prologue* of Proclus' commentary in the *Elements* by Euclid. This *Prologue* transmits the history of Eudemes' geometry, a disciple of Aristotle, fourth century BC. Proclus (412 - 485 AD), neoplatonian philosopher, born in Constantinople, kept this famous historical text. From the beginning of this decisive text, we read: 'We must now talk about the origin of geometry in the present time... We shall say that, according to general tradition, the Egyptians were the first to invent geometry... Thales, the first having been to Egypt, brought back this theory in the Hellad.'

(c) *The modern electronic calculator and the Egyptian scribe: The Rhind Papyrus* starts with a table in which each fraction of the form 2/a is broken down in a sum of fractions of numerator 1, for the values of uneven *a* included between 1 and 100. The calculation, which is complex, leads to a special factorising table, transcribed in the *Rhind Papyrus*. This Egyptian table was used from 1650 BC to Cleopatra, born in Alexandria (69 - 30 BC), and even later till the Western Middle Ages.

The table of the *Rhind Papyrus* is a perfected calculation instrument, remarkable for its elegant and harmonious qualities; electronic calculators have not found any better decomposition than those of the scribe of 1650 BC.

Indeed, in 1967, Professor C.L. Hamblin (University of New South Wales) programmed a computer (KDF-9) at the University of Sydney (Australia) to make a similar calculation. It took the computer five hours to do so, and it produced 22,295 values. The decompositions of the computer were not superior to those of the Egyptian scribe: 'We can conclude that, in this division as elsewhere, the computer did not find a decomposition superior to that given by the ancient scribe' (Richard J. Gillings, *Mathematics in the time of the Pharaohs*, New York, Dover Publications, 1982, p.52; 1st ed., MIT Press, 1972).

These are a few facts in maths, medicine, astronomy and metaphysics which were part of these immense scientific, cultural, and spiritual treasures accumulated by the Egyptians for almost thirty centuries of living history.

In the matter of civilization, the ancient Egyptians did not imitate any other people in antiquity. They themselves invented their writing, their monumental architecture (pyramids, etc.), their literature, their maths, their astronomy, their medicine, their religion, their conception of the world, their arts (painting, sculpture, drawing, carving, music, games, leisure, etc.).

The Egyptian intellectual acquisitions were used for the progress of other people in antiquity, in the glorious path of human civilization: Phoenicians, Hebrews, Greeks, Cretans, Romans, etc., benefited from the positive acquisitions of ancient Egypt and also of Babylonia.

One can closely examine the influence of Egyptian thought upon the birth of Greek thought, particularly since Egypt, in the eyes of all the Greeks, was then considered the most civilized country in the world.

6. Thales of Miletus, pupil of Egyptian priests

Miletus, city of Ionia, in the central part of the coastal region of Asia Minor, was, from the eighth century BC a great commercial metropolis and a powerful focus of Greek culture. Miletus was the seat of the very first Greek philosophical school, the "Ionian School". Therefore, philosophy and science appear in the Greek region of Asia Minor around 600 BC. 'One can see that Greece itself has, at least at the beginning, played no role. The beginnings were in Ionia, particularly in Miletus' (Moses I. Finley, *Les premiers temps de la Grèce: l'âge du bronze et l'époque archaïque*, Paris, Flammarion, 1980, p.166).

Thales (end of 7th century to 6th of sixth century BC) was the founder of this philosophical and scientific school in Miletus. He was the first to be called by the name 'sage' (*oútos prōtos ōnomásthē sophós*). This was when Damasias was archon of Athens in 582.

This first sage from Greece visited Egypt, where he sojourned for a long while to study under the authority of the priests of this African country. 'He learned in Egypt under the direction of priests' (*epaideúthē en Aigúptō hupò tōn hieréōn*).

So, the most ancient representative of Greek philosophy and science (Aristotle affirms that Thales is the founder of natural philosophy: *Metaphysics*, Book I, chap.III) is a former pupil of the Egyptians. Thales brought back from Egypt numerous cosmological, philosophical, mathematical, astronomical knowledge. The influence of Egypt upon Greece with the intermediary of Thales, is consequently real since Thales had no other masters but Egyptian ones.

For Thales the constitutive and primordial matter of the world, the primary elementary principle, was water: 'He placed water at the origin of everything' (*archēn dè tōn pántōn hudōr hupestēsato*).

Thales boldly affirms the unity of matter while defining matter in its simplest form, water, principle of things, beings, of total existing reality. One must note that Thales' water is not the boundless *Okeanos* of Homer, nor the Babylonian waters which surround the earth. Thales puts water, as a principle, at the origin of things.

Nietzsche (1844 - 1900) correctly perceived the way Thales refers to primordial, original water, prime principle of everything. 'Thales saw the unity of being, and when he wished to express it, he talked about water' (F. Nietzsche, *La naissance de la philosophie à l'époque de la tragédie grecque*, Paris, Gallimard, 1938, translated by Bianquis).

Thales' *water* is the Egytian *Noun*. Indeed, the Egyptian *Noun* has a universal meaning. It is the primordial element which speaks to the future, to the whole of nature, through the power of *Râ.* The Egyptian *Noun* is not the boundless ocean of Homer. Neither does it surround the earth and the sky from everywhere as in the Semitic and Sumerian cosmogonies. The Egyptian *Noun* is the basis of the system of physics in ancient Egypt.

Indeed, according to the priests and philosophers of Heliopolis, *Râ* had emerged by himself, of his own energy, from the *Noun,* that is, of the primordial waters. He had engendered, in turn, other divinities, the couple, sky (*Nut*) and earth (*Geb*), separated by air (*Shou*), up to *Osiris* and *Seth, Isis* and *Nephtys*, who had introduced death and resurrection in the world of civilization. It is a sort of vivid theory of *evolution*: first, there is the disorganised matter, *Noun*; then Reason, the organising intelligence, emerges from matter; *Râ* is followed by the formation of the sky (*Nut*) and the earth (*Geb*), their separation by the atmosphere (*Shou*), the genesis of animal, vegetal and human life. *Noun* is in fact an exceptionally rich *concept* : spirit-matter destined for evolution (*kheper*, "to become", in ancient Egyptian). *Râ* is intelligence, the cause of universal arrangement and order. *Râ* is separated from his object. *Râ* is a cosmological factor who works on matter, already "co-existing", *Noun*. *Râ*, the creative intelligence emerged from *Noun*, already announces the *Noûs* of Anaxagoras of Clazomenae (born around 500 BC).

Cicero's (106 - 43 BC) comment concerning Thales' water is quite correct. 'Thales said that everything originated from water; and that from water the mind of God created all things' (Cicero, *The Nature of theGods*, 1,10, 30). Cicero thus illustrates both materialism (water) and spiritualism (god) of Ionian philosophy, while stressing the unity of wholeness as a unity of both living and the divine.

As a matter of fact, the Egyptian *Noun* is exactly a principle of unity; it is matter (water), and *Râ*, the creative intelligence, emerging from this primordial water. Egyptian priests therefore taught Thales an essential discovery: the relation between "the spirit" and all other things, in recognising water as the origin and the prime condition of everything that is.

Indeed, a scientist such as Werner Jaeger convincingly demonstrates that the process of the first Greek thinkers is "theological". One must add that this can be explained by the Egyptian influence on Greek thought, since the beginning of philosophical thought in Greece. The first principle, *Râ*, which has its own divine substance (its *ka*), spurts out of the initial matter, the *Noun*, fluid, homogeneous liquid, at the very beginning. The Egyptian process is essentially "theological", "divine", and at the same time, "materialistic". The birth of theology is also to be found in Egypt (W. Jaeger, *A la naisssance de la théologie. Essai sur les Présocratiques*. Paris, Les

Editions du CERF, 1966, translated from German).

Let us reiterate these important facts:

Ancient Pharaonic Egyptian; *noun,* primordial water.

Coptic (Ancient Egyptian vocalised): *noun,* abyss, abysmal water.

Nuer (Southern Sudan): *noun,* water. One can therefore gather that the native context of Pharaonic philosophy is well and truly in an African, Egypto-Nubian context. Further more, the Pharaonic metaphisycal notions of *ka* and *ba* can be found in the whole of Black Africa.

From Egypt, Thales also learned the notion of the "mobility" of the human soul. 'Thales was the first to demonstrate that the soul (*tēn psychēn*), like nature (*physen*), is always mobile or auto-mobile (*aeì kìnēton ē autokíneton*) '.

Thales is also the first (*protōs*) to have reflected upon these essential questions in Greece: the primordial principle of the constitution of the universe, the mobility of the human soul, geometry, etc.

Indeed, what Thales says of the human soul, is directly owed to Pharaonic anthropology. According to the Egyptians, man was composed of various spiritual forces: *ka,* "the vital force"; *akh,* an immortal, efficacious principle; *ba,* the spiritual part of an individual which recovers its autonomy after death and can move at its liking; the *ren,* the name, which is a living thing, and always expresses direction.

The *ba*, the Egyptian "soul", is not opposed to the "body", as in Christian religion, for instance. The Egyptian *ba* is of a mobile, or automobile nature, a power which is an integrated part of the manifestation of the dead: "Your *ba* is yours, in you; your power is yours, around you" (*The Pyramids Texts*, § 422).

Having studied philosophy in Egypt, Thales could not ignore Egyptian anthropology which conceives of the soul as some living, dynamic, mobile thing; in brief, as a spiritual part of an individual who often prefers to stroll in the fresh air, to rediscover the place where the deceased liked to be during his life.

Being mobile, the "soul" is something which does not die. Indeed, from the earliest times in Egyptian history, one can confirm by the documents (texts and iconography) which attest that something of man, his *ka* (double), his *ba* (soul) survives the death of the body (*khet*). This is why Herodotus, who also sojourned in Egypt, writes with certitude: 'The Egyptians are also the first to state the doctrine that the soul of man is immortal' (Herodotus, II, 123: *prōtoi dè kaì tónde tòn lógon Aigúptioí eisi oi eipóntes, ōs anthrōpou psychē athánatós esti*). Thus, for Herodotus, this metaphysical notion of the "immortality of the human soul", does not originate in Greece, but in Egypt. This is clear.

In Plato's philosophy, the "soul" is a pure spiritual principle, truly distinct from the body, and immortal. In Aristotle's philosophy, the "soul" is united to the body, like a form united to matter, but its spirituality and immortality are less obvious.

Indeed, the term "immortality" only appears for the first time in the *Old Testament* in the Book of Wisdom ("Wisdom of Solomon"), a work written in Greek, around 50 BC; the idea of the immortality of the soul (*pneūma, psychē*), suggested in "The Book of Wisdom" (3:4), is Greek. In fact, the Hebraic *nepeš* (the "self", the "soul") goes towards death, but does not survive as a living being. The immortality of the soul as it is mentioned in the "Book of Wisdom" (3:4) is a product of the Judaism of Alexandria, which was rather hellenised, therefore, an idea really *foreign* to the beliefs and to the psychology of the Hebrews of the Old Testament.

So, before Thales, Plato, Aristotle, before the Jews of Alexandria, before the Hebrews, the ancient Egyptians had already established the idea of the immortality of the human soul, as early as the Ancient Empire (Jacques Pirenne, "*Âme et vie d'outre-tombe chez les égyptiens de l'Ancien Empire*", in "Chronique d'Egypte", Bruxelles, Vol. XXXIV, No. 68, 1959, pp.208-213).

Having learned these ideas in Egypt, Thales was therefore the first Greek to proclaim that 'the soul was of a mobile or auto-mobile nature'. And the poet Choiritos had understood that Thales 'was the first to affirm that the soul is immortal'.

This fundamental notion of Egyptian philosophy is widespread in Black Africa, as we can verify as follows:

Pharaonic Egyptian:	*ba*, "spirit, soul"
Coptic (vocalised Egyptian):	*bai*, "spirit, soul"
Mbochi (Congo):	*ba*, "to be sound in spirit, to be spiritually aware"
Ronga (Mozambique):	*bà, ku-ba* "to be" (sound in spirit)
Mangbetu (North-East Zaire):	*o-bu*, "to be, to exist" (to have one's soul)
Songhay (Niger):	*bi*, "soul, "a being's double"
Bambara (Mali):	*be*, bi "to be, to exist" (to have one's soul, one's spirit)
Greek:	*psychē, pneūma*, "spirit, soul"
Hebrew:	*nepes*, "soul", "self"
Syriac:	*napsā*, "soul"
Arabic:	*nafs*, "soul"
Ethiopian:	*nafs*, "soul"

It is obvious that the Black African world, from Pharaonic Egypt (*ba, bai, be, bi, bu*, etc.), to the Semitic world (*nepeš napsā, nafs,* etc.), the Indo-European world (*pneūma, psychē;* Vedantic Sanskrit (*psu*, "breath, strength"; *a-psu*, "breathless, weakness"); all these cultural worlds are distinct in designating notions as important as soul, vital force, life, immaterial and immortal parts of the soul of the living being, the seat of thoughts, emotions, desires, etc.

Pharaonic philosophy is inseparable from its native, continentental context, i.e., the Black African world; there is not one single fundamental notion of Pharaonic philosophy which is not to be found in Black Africa.

Thales also imported geometry from Egypt to Greece. Herodotus thinks that land-measuring triggered off the *invention* of geometry in Egypt, which

Greeks, such as Thales, later on brought back to their country (Herodotus, II, 109).

The historian of Greek mathematics, Sir Thomas L. Heath, thinks that Thales formulated the preposition: "All diameter cuts the circle into two", after having seen the circle divided in equal sectors which can be found on Egyptian monuments (Sir Thomas L. Heath, *A History of Greek Mathematics*, New York, Dover Publications, 1981, vol I, p.131).

To sum up and to simplify, we have the following comparative chart, to help clarify these ideas:

Ancient Egypt	*Thales of Milletus*
1. Around 2500 BC: construction of the pyramids (geometry, trigono-, metry, astronomy); c. 1850 BC: the *Moscow Payrus* (volume of the trunk of a square-based pyramid; surface of a semi-sphere); c. 1650 BC: the *Rhind Papyrus* with 85 problems copied from an older text (2000 -1800 BC).	1 Thales (c. 640 - 546 BC) founder of Greek geometry, after having studied in Egypt
2. The concept of *Noun*, primordial water, at the origin of everything (*The Pyramid Texts*: 2300 BC).	2. Thales puts water as the principle (*archē*) of everything
3. The metaphysical notions of *ka* and *ba*; the *ba*, mobile soul-bird; concept of the immortality of the human soul.	3. For Thales the soul is always (*aei*)of a mobile or automobile nature.
4. A *Neiloksenos*, a "native of the Nile country", mathematician, explains to Thales the procedure for measuring the height of the	4. Thales determines, in Egypt itself, the height of the pyramid by measuring its shadow.

pyramid according to its shadow,
with the help of a stick (Plutarch,
Le Banquet des Sept Sages, § 147 A).
It is the famous theorem of proportions, which immortalised the name
of Thales.

5. Egyptian astronomers could
"observe" with great exactitude
the eclipses of the sun and of the
moon, and calculate them in
advance in order to calculate, in
the greatest detail and infallibly,
these kinds of phenomena
"(Diodorus Siculus, I, 50). The
eclipses of the sun and of the
the moon were known to the
ancient Egyptians (Serge
Sauneron, *Les prêtes de l'ancienne
Egypte*, Paris, Editions du Seuil,
1959, p.154).

5. Herodotus relates the
prediction of Thales
regarding an eclipse
of the sun occurring in
585 BC. The Egyptian
astronomers certainly
taught Thales how to
predict and
calculate eclipses.

Thales is "the first" to have done this or that in
Greece: the explanation of the constitution of the
universe from a unique substance, conception of the
immortality and of mobility (immateriality) of the
human soul, enunciation of the first elements of
Greek geometry, prediction of eclipses, etc. But
Thales was not the first to have done all this in the
Nile Valley where he sojourned for a long time in his
attempt to inoculate himself with philosophical and
scientific studies (geometry, astronomy).

One can therefore see that philosophy and Greek
sciences originally came from Egypt.

VII. Pythagoras of Samos studied for twenty-two years in Egypt

Dead by 522 BC, Polycrates was the tyrant of Samos (Greek island of the Aegean sea), 533 to 522. He attracted artists and writers to his court, among whom Anacreon, lyric poet, born in Teos (Ionia), in the second half of the sixth century BC. Amasis, King of the twenty-sixth Egyptian dynasty, reigned from 570 to 526 BC. Pythagoras therefore went to Egypt around 558 BC, having been provided with a letter of recommendation from Polycrates to hand to Amasis (Diogenes Laërtius, VIII, 3).

Iamblichus, neoplatonian philosopher, born in Chalcis (c.250 - 330), reports in his biography of Pythagoras that :'He (Pythagoras) stayed for twenty-two years in the Egyptian temples, learning astronomy, geometry, and being initiated in all the sacred ceremonies of the gods' (Iamblichus, *Life of Pythagorus*, 4, 19).

At Heliopolis, Pythagoras received lessons from the Egyptian priest Oinouphis (Plutarch, *Isis and Osiris*, 354 e: *Pythagóran d'Oinoúpheōus Hēuliopolítou.*) *Oinouphis* is the Greek version of the Egyptian name *Wn nfr*, "the good being", one of Osiris' names. Initiated priests could validly carry these names which were divine epithets, formed from religious invocations.

According to Porphyry, neoplatonian philosopher born in Tyre (c. 234-305), Pythagoras had learnt the

Egyptian language and also, obviously, the different forms of Egyptian writing: 'In Egypt, he (Pythagoras) associated with the priests, learned wisdom from them (*tēn sophían*) and also the Egyptian language (*kaì tēn Aiguptíōn phonēn*), on the one hand, and on the other, the three types of writing; epistolographic, hieroglyphic, and symbolic' (Porphyry, *Life of Pythagoras*, 11-12).

Epistolographic writing corresponds to demotic writing and *symbolic* to *hieratic* (sacred) writing. Indeed, Porphyry is correct. There are in fact three types of written Egyptian graphic signs (*tà grámmata*) which correctly form Pharaonic Egyptian writing.

Let us quickly review the Greek testimonies which inform us on the knowledge acquired by Pythagoras in the Nile Valley.

1. **Testimony of Herodotus** (c.484 - 420 BC)

Herodotus links the orphic and pythagorean ceremonies to that of the Egyptian because of the resemblances of rites, of practices, of interdictions (prohibition against woolly clothes). This reveals, for Herodotus, a common origin. This common origin, for Herodotus, is to be found precisely in the religious customs of Egypt (Hérodotus, II, 81).

Chronologically, in fact, Egypt is the mother. Herodotus is certainly right to assert that pythagoreanism has common traits with orphism: revelations, progressive initiation, ritual purification, all

the things which hold such an important place in
Egypt.

Still, according to Herodotus, Pythagoras formulated
the doctrine of metempsychosis from Egyptian data
(Herodotus, II, 123).

2. Testimony of Isocrates (436 - 338 BC)

Isocrates relates that Pythagoras greatly admired,
as many other Greeks, the devotion of Egyptians: 'He
(Pythagoras) came to Egypt and became the
disciple (*mathētēs*) of the people over there, he was
the first to bring back to Greece all the philosophy
(*tēn t'állēn philosophían prōtos eis toùs Hellēnas
ekómisen*) and became the most prominent for his
interest in sacrifices (*perì tàs thusìas*) and in the
ceremonies of the sanctuaries' (Isocrates, Busiris, XI,
28).

According to Isocrates, Pythagoras, disciple of the
Egyptians, had learned in Egypt all the philosophy he
then brought back to Greece. One can see that the
Egyptian (African) origin of Greek philosophy is an
historical fact, admitted as such by the Greeks
themselves, in antiquity.

The "taste for mystery" of Pythagoras and
pythagoreans equally comes directly from Egypt,
where the divine sanctuaries, with secret
architectures, harboured even more secret practices
of the priests, themselves initiated in the great
mysteries of the gods. Pythagoras most probably knew

the sacred rites of the Nile Valley, for he spent twenty-two years of his life there, being a hard working pupil, a disciple of Egyptian priests, his masters.

3. Plutarch's testimony (c.50 - 125)

Plutarch relates that 'Pythagoras was full of admiration for Egyptian priests who also admired him...' (Plutarch, *Isis and Osiris*, 354, e-f: *máltista d'outos, ōs éoike, thaumastheìs kaì thaumásas toùs ándras*).

Hieroglyphic writing is full of sacred science. This sacred science was not really disclosed by Egyptian priests. But in Pythagoras' case, this sacred science must have been taught to him, the Greek pupil so much admired by Egyptian scientists. This is why most pythagorean precepts are in no way inferior to hieroglyphic writings: 'There are indeed no differences between the texts called hieroglyphics, and most pythagorean precepts' (Plutarch, *Isis and Osiris*, 354, f: *tōn gàr kalouménōn hieroglyphikōn grammátōn oudèn apoleípei tà pollà tōn Pythagorikōn parangelmátōn*).

Indeed, hieroglyphic signs express quite a philosophy of writing. For instance, by representing the *sun*, not by a *circle* (with or without rays) but by a *scarab*, hieroglyphic writing becomes an enigmatic representation which refers directly to Egyptian mythology and philosophy. The *scarab* is a symbol which treats and conceals a profound teaching, enigmatically. It is therefore in a secret, hidden manner, that Egyptian initiates revealed the principles of things.

Pythagoras certainly fulfilled all the conditions to be initiated to the sacred science of Egyptian priests; ritual circumcision, learning of the Egyptian language and patience.

And surely it is not in vain that Plutarch, who himself visited Egypt, should clearly attribute an Egyptian origin to pythagorean symbolism: 'I also believe for myself (*dōkō d'égōge*), that pythagoreans in calling Apollo the monad, Artemis the dyad, Athena the septenary, and Poseidon the first cube, wanted to imitate what is inscribed on Egyptian temples (*toîs epì tōn hierōn hidruménois*), what is practised there (*kaì glyphoménois*), and also, by Zeus!, what can be seen engraved...' (*kaì graphoménois*, Plutarch, *Isis and Osiris*, 354, f).

Indeed, Pythagoras saw what is inscribed on Egyptian temples, the great sacred writing, the beautifully engraved hieroglyphics, sometimes in colour, as well as the practice of ceremonies and other divine rites. But how did Pythagoras really imitate Egyptian priests in calling divinities by numbers?

Let us take an example: in the ceremonies of Osiris, god is hieroglyphically represented by a seat, an eye, and whose statue is tightly wrapped in his skintight garment, his arms crossed on his chest, grasping the sceptre and the flail, his head covered with the white mitre between two big feathers, also reveal a symbolism of numbers. How? Because the ceremonies of Osiris, god of the earth and of vegetal forces, took place at the beginning of the fourth month (*khoiak*) of the Egyptian year, when the waters of the flood would recede. On the other hand, Osiris was born on the first day of the five complementary days of the year. And Diodorus Siculus reports that all the colleges of the priests revered 'the tomb of Osiris and the 360 urns which are deposited there' (Diodorus Siculus, 1, 22). Let us finally recall that the *first day of the New Year* was symbolically related to the potter god, Khnoum. In Egypt, there is quite a philosophical and cosmogonical symbolism linked to numbers, to their power. In the Cairo museum, an inscription on a relief of Ramses II's temple can be read as follows: 'This temple is like the sky in all its proportions'.

4. Testimony of Porphyry (234 - 305)

Porphyry relates that in antiquity, geometry had interested the Egyptians (*geōmetrías mèn gàr ek palaiōn chrónōn epimelēthēnai Aiguptíous*: Porphyry, *op. cit.*, 6).

After Pythagoras' arrival in Egypt, with Polycrates' letter of recommendation, Pharaoh Amasis asked the priests to meet him: 'After mingling with those (priests) of Heliopolis, he was sent to Memphis to older priests, and from Memphis, he arrived to those of Diospolis' (Porphyry, *ibid,*, 7).

In Egypt, Pythagoras studied in *Heliopolis* (in ancient Egyptian *Iounou, Iwnw,* in the Bible, *On*), north-east of present day Cairo; in *Memphis* (in ancient Egyptian *Ankh-taoui,* and since the Middle Empire *Men-nefer,* which gave Memphis in Greek) on the Nile, upstream from the Delta; finally in Diospolis (in fact Diospolis Magna, that is, Thebes, city of the gods and of the living, Diospolis Parva being the city of *Heou,* outside the great bend of the Nile).   Luxor (in Pharaonic Egyptian *Nut,* "the city", or *Ouaset* (*Waset*), in the Bible *No,* in Greek Thebes or Diospolis Magna, city of Zeus, that is, of Amon; and in Karnak, north of Luxor, marks the spot of the most international city in the whole of Mediterranean antiquity.   We can safely say then that Pythagoras went to the *best* Egyptian schools, in Heliopolis, in Memphis, in Thebes, from 558 - 536 BC.

Porphyry, summarising Diogenes (c.100 BC), relates that in Egypt, Pythagoras mingled with the priests, learned their wisdom, the Egyptian language, and the three types of writing (*kaì tēn sophían eksémathe kaì tēn Aiguptíōn phōnén, grammátōn dè trissàs diaphorás*).

In other words, Pythagoras knew Egyptian philosophy from within, having studied in various priestly colleges, among the most famous of the country, having learned the indigenous language, Egyptian. This is why the Egyptian relationship to the pythagorean school is undeniable.

In Egypt Pythagoras' theorem follows from the known

observation, according to which the square of the side which supports the right angle is equal to the square of the sides which include the right angle.

So, more than twenty centuries before the famous Pythagorean theorem, Egyptian geometricians of the Ancient Empire had applied this theorem, in placing Cheops' sepulchral chamber, which is a rectangle parallelepiped, at the precise level where the surface of the pyramid is equal to half of its base. In doing so, the Egyptians correctly applied this general knowledge: that the diagonal of a square of a given surface is equal to the side of a square of twice the surface. This property of the diagonal of the square is a particular case of the hypothenuse of any rectangle triangle.

On the other hand, the property stated by Pythagoras' theorem was known to the Egyptians, for the triangle whose sides are measured by the numbers 3, 4, 5, etc.: Egyptian geometricians used a similar triangle to construct on the ground a perpendicular to a given straight line.

The triangular paving of Egyptian temples, which are tiles formed of isoceles rectangle triangles, give an idea of Pythagoras' theorem, for it is a particular application of this theorem with rectangle triangles whose cathetus are equal. The sacred Egyptian triangle 3, 4, 5, will become the cosmic triangle of the pythagorean school.

One also attributes to Pythagoras the discovery of *irrational numbers*. It is generally accepted that the study of irrational numbers was born of the study of the relation between the diagonal of the square and its side. The Egyptians knew irrational numbers. Thus the scribe Ahmes (around 1650 BC) established the value of *pi* (π) to 3.1605, in drawing a circle in a square, and in subtracting from the surface of this square, the surface of the triangles determined by the drawing of the circle. This graphic method enabled one to be aware of the approximation regarding the tracings.

Significantly, this awareness of approximation regarding the tracings is at the origin of the discovery of irrational numbers. On the other hand, the manipulation of whole numbers, of fractions, of decimals and of a series of multiples of 3, 4, 5, for the formation of rectangle triangles and the setting of the right angle, allowed the Egyptians to obtain approximations of irrational relations rigorous enough to get the most delicate, regulating tracings.

The central idea of pythagorean arithmetic is that *everything is number (tòn mèn dē kósmon o Pythagóras metrēi:* 'Pythagoras measures the world'). Everything is explained by the number. To know is, in the end, to determine and interpret numerical relations. Numbers are the sovereign direction of the cosmos. For Pythagoras and pythagoreans, rational speculation and mysticism are linked.

Actually, in Egypt, the notion of cosmic harmony, *Maât,* is absolutely fundamental. This cosmic harmony is reflected in the agreements among the

Universe, the Temples and Man. Thus, the central idea of the initial pedagogy conveyed by pythago-reanism originates in Egypt.

Vorille's work and especially that of de Lubicz on Egyptian temples and their symbolism, emphasise the relation between the proportions of Egyptian temples and those of the human body. Pythagoras brought back from Egypt to Greece an important geometrical corpus which was designed in Egypt to the needs of the engineer, the architect, and the sculptor.

Finally, Pythagoras is considered as the inventor of the diatonic scale (see Theon de Smyrne, beginning of the second century AD, author of a treaty of music,*Musique*, chapter IX, X and XI). Modualtion or the diatonic scale usually goes up in tones and also shows some vigour and firmness.

In fact, at the end of the 19th century, the French Egyptologist Victor Loret, had studied the Egyptian system of tonality, using as data around thirty flutes kept in museums. He had measured these instruments to a tenth of a millimetre of the inside diameter, the distance from the holes to the mouthpiece, the shape and the dimensions of these holes, etc. He had played these instruments with the help of physics, oboe and flute teachers of the Conservatoire de Lyon. Victor Loret was therefore able to establish the musical scale provided by these instruments of Ancient Egypt. This was truly a meticulous, patient, exhaustive task.

Here is Victor Loret's conclusion: 'We can record

here one more example to support the opinion of those who see a pharaonic origin to most Greek sciences: the major scale given by a great number of ancient flutes from Egypt is Pythagoras' diatonic scale' (Victor Loret, *Les flûtes egyptiennes antiques*, in *Journal Asiatique*, Paris, 8th series, Vol.XIV, No. 2, septembre - octobre 1989, pp.11-228).

In any case, the diatonic scale was played and taught in Egypt twenty centuries before Pythagoras' birth. In the Ancient Empire, *Khufu-Ankh* is a singer, flute player and musical inspector: he died under the reign of the Pharoah Ouserkaf (2450 - 2442 BC). *Khufu-Ankh* is the *first musician* known of in universal history. He played at the Court of King Ouserkaf (5th dynasty) and occupied the position of singer, of director of singers, and flute player. He obtained permission for erecting his tomb near Gizeh's (Giza) pyramids (Hans Hickmann, *Musicologie Pharaonique*, Khel/Rhin, Heitz, 1956).

Summary

* Pythagoras studied in Egypt for twenty-two years, in Heliopolis, in Memphis, and in Thebes. His teacher in Heliopolis was the Egyptian priest *Oinouphis* (Ounouphis);

* In Egypt, Pythagoras learnt the Egyptian language, writing, geometry, philosophy (wisdom), mysteries, the notion of the power of the number, music (the diatonic scale), and astronomy;

✻ Pythagoras underwent ritual circumcision in Egypt in order to be admitted to the temples to learn astronomy, geometry and to be initiated in all the sacred ceremonies of the gods (Iamblichus, and Clement of Alexandria in *Stromata*, Book I, chapter XV, 66: *kaì perietémneto*, 'and he was circumcised').

This is well and truly the circumcision of some African rituals, a significant trait of the cultural identity of black people. This cultural identity between the Nile Valley and the rest of Black Africa is not only obvious when it comes to the fact, but also to the terms. To demonstrate this:

Pharaonic Egyptian	:	*s^{c}b, sâb, sbi*, "to circumcise"
Coptic (vocalised Egyptian)	:	*sĕbbĕ*, "to circumcise"
Kikongo (Bantu, Central Africa):		*seba*, "to circumcise", "to cut", "to wound lightly with a knife"
Bemba (Bantu, Zambia)	:	*ku-sèbà, sèbà*, "to cut" (grass)
Arabic (Semitic)	:	*hatana*, "to circumcise".

In ancient Egypt the verb *s^{c}b, sâb, sbi*, "to circumcise," had a ritual meaning, and circumcision was practised in a group; *iw s^{c}b.i hn^c s 120*, "When I was circumcised with 120 men", which one can read on the stela of Henout-sen (first Intermediate Period: 2190 - 2050 BC). This compares with identical age-group circumcision in Black Africa.

Pythagoras, whose doctrine, founded on the knowledge of number and on the meaning of universal harmony, experienced a long adventure, first with his immediate disciples, Archippus and Clinias, Archytas of Tarentum, Philolaos, Simmias, Cebes and Lysis, Eurytos; then with Pindar and Plato; then pythagoreanism reached Rome towards the end of the fourth century, and was favoured by Appius Claudius Caecus, Scipios the African, and Cato. The research of Diogenes Laertius, of Porphyry, and of Iamblichus on Pythagoras, are more testimonies of the vitality of pythagoreanism in the third century. Pythagoras, a pupil of the Egyptians, made the Greeks benefit from the treasures gathered on the banks of the Nile: the destiny of man, as well as on the constitution of the universe.

VIII. Plato's Egyptian Lesson (427 - 447 BC)

1. Plato studied in Egypt

Hermodores of Syracuse, a direct disciple of Plato, who was a member of the academy as a specialised professor during Plato's last ten years, tells us: 'At the age of twenty-eight, Plato *(éipeita genómenos oktōn kaì éikosin etōn)*, went to Megara, to see Euclid, accompanied by a few other pupils of Socrates. Then Plato went to Cyrene, to see the mathematician Theodorus and to his home in Italy, to Philalaos and Eurytos, both pythagoreans; then to Egypt, to see the prophets *(énthen te eís Aígupton parà toùs prophētas)* '. Plato therefore went on a study trip in the Nile Valley, to be taught by Egyptian priests. This very precious information comes from one of his immediate disciples when Plato himself was still alive. Plato studied notably in Heliopolis, under priest Sekhnouphis, and in Memphis under Knouphis (Clement ofAlexandria, *Stromata,* Book I, ch. XI, 69).

2. Plato "egyptianises" words instead of "grecifying" them.

Saīs, transcribed by Plato as Sais, corresponds to the Egyptian *S3w, Saou.* Mentioned since the beginning of the Ancient Empire, Sais, 30 km northeast of Tanta on the Delta, on the Rosetta branch of the Nile, was a high place of Neith's cult.

Neith, transcribed as *Nēith* by Plato, corresponds to the Egyptian *Nt,* the Egyptian goddess called *Athēnā* by the Greeks (Plato, *Timaeus,* 21 e).

Theuth of Plato, equals *Djhouty* in Egyptian, and in Coptic *Thoout, Thōt, Thaut,* inventor and divine protector of arts, laws and science: this Egyptian god was assimilated to *Hermes* by the Greeks. Plato does not use the word *Hermes* like other Greek writers (Plutarch, for example) but the Egyptian word *Djhouty, Thōt,* which he writes as *Theuth.*

Plato's *Thamous,* a king who ruled the whole of Egypt and whose capital was Thebes, city of the god Amon *(Phaedrus,* 274 d), certainly refers to *Thoutmes,* in Egyptian *Djhouty-mes* ("Thot is born"), the name of the four kings of the eight dynasty who made Thebes famous, as Amon did for Karnak.

When Plato mentions Egyptian products, he obviously

retains the indigenous words, *kiki*, "oil" (*Timaeus*, 60 a) corresponds to the Egyptian *k3k3, kyky, kiki* in Coptic, meaning "castor" and "caster oil". The word "ibis", Thot's sacred bird, is obviously an Egyptian word.

In *Phaedrus*, we have this series: Naucratis and Thebes, Theuth and Amon, King Thamous, the sacred ibis bird.

In *Timaeus*, we have another series: Sais, Neith, King Amasis, the priests of Sais.

In the *Laws*, Isis is summoned, and in *Philebus*, Theuth. One can easily verify that Plato had a knowledge of places, gods, men, and Egyptian symbols (the ibis bird).

3. For Plato, Egypt is the country of the highest antiquity

In Egypt, since most ancient antiquity, everything was recorded in the temples. Human memory, constantly supported by writing and by written documents themselves, is consequently well established on the banks of the Nile. It is in this way that Plato considers Egypt as a comprehensive archaeological reservoir of universal history. Egypt is the country of knowledge lit up by time (*Timaeus*, 22 b 23 a).

Solon's memory does not go back very far in time: 'Solon, Solon, you Greeks are still children (*aeì pãidés este*); and there is no such thing as an old Greek.' (Plato, *Timaeus*, 22 b).

The Greeks therefore had valid reasons to go and learn ancient knowledge in Egypt.

4. Egypt is the Cradle of Writing and Sciences

In *Phaedrus*, Socrates explains that the truth (*tò alēthès*), is known by the elders. Justifiably so, because Socrates had heard from the elders (*tōn protérōn*) that near Naucratis, in Egypt, the divinity represented by the sacred emblem of the ibis, Theut, was at the origin of civilization and science: Theut was the first to discover the science of number (*arithmón*), calculus (*logismòn*), geometry (*geō-metrían*), astronomy (*astronomían*), backgammon (*petteías*), dices (*kubeías*), and finally and especially writing (*grámmata*; Plato, *Phaedrus*, 274 c-d.).

For the Greeks, before Socrates' birth, there was no possible doubt: Egypt was indeed, in their eyes, the cradle of science and technology, of games, of writing, in short, of written and scientific civilization.

This is by now an old Greek tradition, held as true by the Greeks themselves, and which Socrates revives in *Phaedrus*. Established Greek tradition does not think the same of the antiquities of Mesopotamia. For the enlightened Greeks, the antiquities of Egypt constitute the very cradle of human civilization, the origin of the whole intellectual and cultural development of humanity around the Mediterranean.

5. Egypt is a Perfect Model of Artistic and Intellectual Organization

The cultural exception which distinguishes Egypt in the eyes of Plato is that this country is the only one where art is legislated. Codified in this way, art (sculpture, painting, music, dance, etc.) can therefore play a legitimately high social and moral function and thus its pedagogic role is irreplaceable. This clearly comes under the heading of the *Laws*. The beautiful figures (*kalà schēmata*) and the nice melodies (*tà mélē*) are rigorous, "exemplary" models, strictly forbidden to revolutionise (*kainotomēin*) or to imagine (*epinoeīn*) in an illusory manner, other models contrary to ancestral canons (*tá patria*), contrary to *Maât.*

Plato states a fact that he finds admirable and that is the antiquity of Egyptian art, its hieratism, its conservatism, its tradition, and above all its ontological function: 'Plato shows himself as being enamoured of hieratic art, immutable as that which he had admired in the Nile Valley' (Pierre-Maxime Schuhl, *Platon et l'art de son temps (arts plastiques)*, Paris, P.U.F., 1952, p.XV).

This is in fact a highly philosophical problem: the strict regulation of art, the calendar established according to the festivals of the gods, the consecration of every dance and music, and the educative Egyptian methods, fed Plato' s politics. (*The Laws*, VII, 799 a-b).

6. Egypt has the Best Method to teach Maths to Children

In *The Laws,* a work written between 370 - 347 BC, Plato demonstrates the greatest interest for the Egyptian pedagogy of mathematics. This is because method is primordial for Plato. It is more dangerous to learn with a bad method (*metà kakēs agōgēs*) than to ignore. Ignorance, even total and profound, in any subject, is never so dangerous, nor greatly catastrophic: 'It is much more dangerous, on the contrary, to have learned a lot and to know a lot without a method' (*The Laws,* VII, 819 a).

7. Plutarch applied himself to conciliate Egyptian Philosophy with Plato's

The most enlightened (*oi sophōtatoi*) among the Greeks (*tōn Hellēnōn*) who studied in Egypt are: Solon, Thales, Plato, Eudoxus, Pythagoras (Plutarch, *Isis and Osiris,* 354 e).

For Plutarch, the Egyptian myth of Osiris and Seth constitutes the historical explanation of Plato's doctrine: 'And Plato, although often expressing himself in an obscure and veiled manner, names one of these opposing principles, the "same", and the other, the "other" (*Isis and Osiris,* 370 f).

Osiris is the same, the identity, and Seth the other, the difference. The origin and the composition of the world is the product of a mixture of these two opposing forces, and the best one of the two prevails. Osiris is the soul of the world, Seth the body of the world: 'In the soul of the world, intelligence and reason are the guide, and the sovereign master of all which is excellent, is Osiris' (*Isis and Osiris*, 371 a: *en mèn oūn tē psychē noūs kaì lógos o tōn arístōn pántōn hēgemōn kaì kyrios Osirís estin*).

In fact, in *Timaeus* (35 q), the indivisible essence is the soul of the world, while the divisible essence is the body of the universe.

To sum up, for Plutarch, the whole discussion of Plato on the world comes directly from Egypt. It is for this reason, valid in his eyes, that Plutarch associates the philosophy of the Egyptians with that of Plato's, which can be historically justified since Plato studied in Egypt with the priests. Plutarch then analyses platonian philosophy in the light of Egyptian thought (Plutarch, *Isis and Osiris*, 370 a - 384 a).

IX. Conclusion

The relations between Egypt and ancient Greece are of great importance, especially in order to understand, primarily, the birth and the unfolding of Greek sciences and philosophies.

The etymology of the word "*sophós* ", "wise", "*sophiá*", "wisdom", is not established, either in Indo-European, or in Greek itself. Logically then, one should look for this etymology in the Egyptian language: *sbō, sabē*, "wise", "learned".

Around 2000 BC an Egyptian text already gives an ample and astonishing definition of the *sage*. It is difficult to separate the origin of Greek philosophy from its "oriental" and African context, notably Pharaonic Egyptian. From Thales to the School of Alexandria, including Solon, Pythagoras, Xenophanes, Anaxagoras, Empedocles, Democritus, Plato, Aristotle, one can clearly demonstrate the influence of Egyptian thought on the Greeks.

Under the Pharaohs of the twenty-sixth dynasty, there were many Greeks in the Valley of the Nile, notably in the great centres such as Sais, Heliopolis, Memphis, and Thebes (Luxor). One had to pay to travel from Greece to Egypt, following either the Oriental or Western route.

In the Valley of the Nile, the Greek students could learn theology, geometry, astronomy, medicine, the mysteries of life and death, cosmogony, cosmic harmony, the arts, morality, and wisdom.

We have insisted to a slight extent on Thales of Miletus, the first philosopher of the Greek world, on Pythagoras of Samos, whose influence was so great in antiquity, and on Plato of Athens, whose powerful work is still participating in the education of the cultural consciousness of the whole Western world (including their former European colonies, globally). These three Greek philosophers who significantly contributed to humanity, studied in the Valley of the Nile — Pythagoras for twenty years, according to his best biographer.

This is history. And the correct history must be done with "objectivity" (a somewhat over abused word), and a critical spirit. A true "objective", critical history of Greek philosophy reveals many of its roots in African philosophy. The late Cheikh Anta Diop, one of the greatest pioneers in the study of comparative histories and cultures, had emphasised this.

APPENDIX: QUESTIONS

1. The Greek word *sophós*, "one who knows, who masters an art or a technique", "educated, intelligent", has the derivative *sophía*, "ability to do", "practical wisdom" and also "wisdom in general"; we also have *tó sophón*, "science, wisdom", and the denominative verb, *sophóō*, "instruct". Hence the compound of progressive dependence which is: *philó* — "who loves", *tò sophón*, "science, wisdom", hence *philosophía*, "liking for science, wisdom". Whereas the word *sophós* has no etymology; it exists neither in Indo-European nor in Greek itself. What can motivate or justify the derivation of the Greek word *sophós* from the ancient Egyptian *sbō, sabe, seba*, "educated", "intelligent, wise"?

2. Isocrates (436 - 338 BC) considers Egypt as the birthplace of medicine and philosophy. Aristotle (384 - 322 BC) held Egypt as the birthplace of mathematical arts, that is to say, of geometry, the science of numbers (arithmetic) and astronomy. Why?

3. What is the first definition of the sage, the philosopher, in the cultural and scientific history of humanity? Justify your answer through elaboration.

4. According to Greek tradition itself, who are the cultivated Greeks who went to the Nile Valley to learn from Egyptian priests?

5. In order to go from Greece to Egypt, which routes could the Greeks follow? And, according to Socrates, what was the cost of the journey?

6. What could the Greeks learn in the Nile Valley? Develop your answer.

7. Thales of Miletus (end of 7th century - beginning of 6th century BC) is the founder of the first philosophical and scientIfIc school in Greece. He remained in Egypt in order to study. What influence, if any, did Egypt have on him? Present a comparative picture.

3

GENETIC LINGUISTIC CONNECTIONS:
ANCIENT EGYPT & BLACK AFRICA

1 Which scientific discipline does this matter concern?

t concerns *historical linguistics*, also referred to as comparative or evolutionary linguistics. By this fact, it is also a matter of cultural linguistics. The following exemplifies this:

Not one single scholar in the world has ever established direct links of an historical order between Germanic people (German, English, etc.) and ancient Greeks. Nevertheless, all the people who naturally speak Germanic languages (German, Dutch, English, etc.) consider ancient Greece as their own cultural base. This is because of the Indo-European linguistic and genetic link which means that

Germanic, Slav, Latin, Greek, Hittite, etc., derive from a common predialectal ancestor, namely the "Indo-European", which is only the result of historical linguistic reconstruction. With the help of geography, Greco-Latin antiquity became the classical antiquity of Europe, that is to say, a precious heritage, and on a solid base with Judaeo-Christianity and Western civilization, up to its most modern aspects. European cultural consciousness maintains a huge space formed precisely by antiquity, not the Meso-potamian, but the Greco-Latin, rightly considered as their own antiquity. Everything else: Chinese, Indian, African, Precolombian, and Oceanian antiquities belong to the cultural and historical heritage of humanity. The West does not identify with Chinese antiquity even if they are studied and taught in the West. And it was not an accident that the European Economic Community chose Athens as the cultural capital of Europe.

In the same manner, on the African side, one should not hesitate to draw all the consequences of the genetic and linguistic link of ancient Egyptian, Coptic, and modern African languages.

2. The method of historical linguistics

These are the main axioms of comparative histori-cal or evolutionary linguistics:

(a) Human languages develop and change: diachronic linguistics precisely studies the successive modification of language and its evolution.

(b) The evolutionary rhythm of languages is rather slow and a language develops even if it is not written: a language has an oral tradition independently of writing. For instance, Latin appears in history in mid-third century BC, to develop and die with Roman Latin, from the fifth to the eight centuries AD. Nothing prevents us from including Latin and Lithuanian (a Baltic language) in the Indo-European comparison, even if Lithuanian is only attested to in history from the fifteenth century: Latin: *sum* (a repair), *es, est;* Lithuanian: *esmi, esi, êsti,* " I am", "you are", "he/she *is* ".

(c) The object of synchronic linguistics is to study the system of a language as it works at a given moment. In reality, diachronic and synchronic linguistics interlock.

(d) The comparative method restores the main outlines of the predialectal mother tongue, the common predialectal language, by comparing and examining sounds (phonetics), the form of the words and of grammar (morphology, syntax), the lexicological facts (vocabulary), common to the words and grammar, the lexicological facts common to the different attested languages which are, in fact, different forms taken during the course of time, by a unique original language.

The comparative method shows that a language is rarely isolated in time and space, that is to say, that it is rare to come across a language which does not belong to a more or less large community, family or

group, that is not more or less ancient. This be-
longing of a language to a family is interpreted by
profound similarities which are not fortuitous, nor
acquired by borrowing words. They must be
correspondences, similarities, resemblances which
rest upon basic and inherited facts.

As we have seen, the method is comparative and
inductive. One starts from the instruction of the
similarities and differences between the attested and
compared languages, to demonstrate their
common origin. So, languages that are today
distinctive, derive from a uniquely common
language if continuity is more or less established
between the compared languages.

Regarding the subject of genetic linguistic links,
Emile Benveniste further clarifies the methodology:
'The proof of the link consists of regular similarities,
defined by correspondences, between complete
forms, morphemes, and phonemes' (Emile Benveniste, *Problems de Linguistique Generale*, Paris,
Gallimard, 1966, p.101).

It is obvious that series are imperative and that
random coincidences must be discarded, also
borrowings and the effects of convergence. The
presumption of link is acquired if the proof is
convincing: 'So, the correspondence between Latin
est: *sunt*, German *ist*: *sind*, and French *est*: *sont*,
suggests, at the same time, phonetic equations, the
same morphological structure, the same alternation,
the same classes of verbal forms and the same
meaning' (Emile Benveniste, *Ibidem*).

The example given by Benveniste is quite Indo-European:

Hittite (2nd millenium BC):	*ešmi*	Sanskrit:	*ásmi*
	ešši		*ási*
	ešzi		*ásti*

Greek	: *emí*	Latin:	*sum*
	eī	(Dorian *essí*)	*es*
	estí		*est*

All these forms originally rest upon the Indo-European + *esmi*, + *esi* + *esti*, forms which are rebuilt by comparison and induction.

Let us take another example. The Greek word *drus*, tree, originally rests upon an Indo-European theme + *dru-*, with a short *u*: it refers to the name of a "tree", the meaning "oak" being secondary. It is because the oak is not an Indo-European tree. Other languages bring these testimonies: Indo-Iranian *dāru*, "tree"; old Slav, *drěwo*, "tree"; Gothic, *triu*, "tree"; Anglo-Saxon, *Treow* "tree"; English, *tree*. The Greek *dendron* is a reduplication. It is difficult for a language to borrow a word such as tree from another. This word is therefore inherited.

From these attested forms:

Sanskrit	: *páti-*,	"husband, master"
Avestic	: *paiti-*,	"husband, master"
Tokharian A	: *pats*,	"husband"
Tokharian B	: *petso*,	"husband"
Greek	: *pósis, pósios*,	"husband" (that is to say, head of the household)

Latin	: potis	"powerful", "who can"
Lithuanian	: *pàts*	(from an ancient *patis*), "husband'
Latvian (Baltic)	: *pats,*	"husband"

This linguistic reasoning results in posing this predialectal, unique common form of Indo-European origin: + *potis*, "husband", "master".

An Indo-European root word: + *mer-*, "to die", has taken different historical forms in time and space: Sanskrit: *mriyáte* (*mrtá-*, "death"); Avestic: *mərəta-*, "death"; Latin: *morior* (*mortuus*); old Slav: *mĭro* (*mrŭtvŭ*, "death"); Lithuanian: *miřštu*. The likelihood of a language borrowing the word "die" from another is obviously improbable. It is well and truly a lexeme inherited from a predialectal common ancestor.

An old root-name of Indo-European origin: + *domo*, "house" (built), "dwelling", gave, in history: Sanskrit, *dáma*, "house"; old Slav, *domŭ;* Russian, *dom;* Latin, *domus;* Provençal *doma;* French, *domicile* (from the Latin word *domicilium*, abbreviation for *domus*); Italian *duono* (hence the French *dôme*: the dôme of Milan, that is to say, the cathedral; English *king-dom*, "realm" (= the King's abode, King's domaine); Greek *dómos*, "dwelling", "house".

With these few examples: + *domo* -, + *mer* -, + *potis*, + *dru*, + *esmi*, we can see how they were carried into attested historical languages. A genetic link connects all historical forms derived from the original common forms. Indeed, each element of expression of a word in a language, is linked by a function to an element of expression from other languages of comparison. And the function of each element is naturally conditioned by its surrounding and by the position it occupies in the word.

In these examples, we insisted above all, on lexicology and vocabulary facts. It is quite a pertinent level of comparison.

3. Can one apply the method of historical linguistics, which is comparative and inductive, to black African languages considered to be without writing?

Linguistic science is not less universal than other sciences. The comparative and inductive method of general and historical linguistics is applicable to all the languages of the world, including, of course, black African languages.

It is also obvious that the pedigree of a scholar like Emile Benveniste can be summarised as follows: the method is well known. It has been tested in establishing more than one linguistic family. The Indo-European, the Common Semitic, etc.

It can well be applied to languages without history, without writing, whatever their structure. This fertile method is neither limited to any type of languages nor to any region of the world. 'There are no reasons', concludes Benveniste, 'to think that "exotic" or "primitive languages" should require other comparative criteria *different* from those required for Indo-European or Semitic languages' (Emile Benveniste, *op.cit.,* pp.101-102).

It is therefore quite legitimate, in the field of linguistic science, to apply the comparative and inductive method of historical linguistics to black African languages, to Coptic and Pharaonic Egyptian, in order to demonstrate whether or not these languages are genetically linked. One has to lay down the criteria.

4. Criteria for comparing Pharaonic Egyptian and modern Black African languages

These criteria are essential and operational:

(a) Language has an oral tradition independent of writing. The Latin of the 3rd century BC and the Lithuanian of the 16th, both present, however remote in time or space, a faithful picture of Indo-European. We can therefore compare Egyptian and Coptic forms with correspondences in modern black African forms, even if we do not have all the successive stages of black African languages in the written form.

Leonard Bloomfield's (1887 - 1949) book, *Language,* is the basis of the American structuralist school, and in it he compared, genetically and historically, four principal languages of the Algonquin central group: *Fox, Ojibway, Cree,* and *Menomini.* He was therefore able to demonstrate with reconstructed forms of attested languages, *Primitive Central Algonguin* or proto-Algonquin, but the American linguistic scholar did not possess any previous recordings or documents for the four compared languages ('for which we have no older records': Leonard Bloomfield, *Language*, edition of 1965, pp. 359-360; first edition 1933).

(b) The criteria of comparison are guaranteed by Pharaonic Egyptian which is the oldest witness of compared languages. So the big time span between Pharaonic Egyptian and modern black African languages, instead of being a handicap, is, conversely, a strong criteria for comparison which must always make sure of some ancient facts for certain compared languages. This means that it is linguistically and historically less interesting to compare, for instance, the *Fongbe* (Abomey, Bénin) and the *Yoruba* (Nigeria, West Africa), but it is more pertinent to compare, for instance, *Pharaonic Egyptian* and *Yoruba.* Indeed, the oldest Egyptian hieroglyphic texts date back to around 3000 years BC and the first written forms of Coptic as early as the third century BC.

(c) Consequently, the enormous geographical discontinuity strongly favours the exclusion of borrowing in these ancient times on the whole established, morphological, phonetical, and lexicological concordances.

That is to say, that the very old separation between the *Egyptian* and *Yoruba languages,* from the common predialectal block, eliminates the effects of convergence, and random, haphazard borrowing:

1. Pharaonic Egyptian : *mi* "take"
   Coptic (vocalised : *mo, ma,* "take"
      Egyptian)
   Yoruba : *mú,* "take"

2. Pharaonic Egyptian : *mw,* "water"
   Coptic : *mo, mē,* "water"
   Yoruba : *o-mi, omi,* "water" (Bini, Edo : *a-mē, amē*)

3. Pharaonic Egyptian : *dj.t,* "cobra"
   Coptic : *adjō, ĕdjō,* "viper"
   Yoruba : *ejò, edjò,* "snake"

4. Pharaonic Egyptian : *ir.t,* "eye"
   Coptic : *ĕyĕr, yĕr,* "eye"
   Yoruba : *ri,* "to see"

It would be very fortunate indeed if all these Egyptian and Yoruba forms, identical on the basis of inherited lexemes, came by pure chance.

If connections and serial links are established between Pharaonic Egyptian, Coptic and modern Black African languages, one is consequently compelled to recognise a familiarity, a knock-on effect (as the expressesion goes for plants), even if one drifts further away from the initial type, that is to say, from the prototypes which are only rebuilt by linguistic reasoning. Thus, Tokharian B *petso,* Greek *posis, posios,* Lithuanian *pàts* (*patis*), take us back to this unique predialectal form of Indo-European: + *potis.*

5. "Hamito-Semitic" or "Afro-Asiatic": a persisting scientific hoax

The linguistic domain of "Hamito-Semitic" or "Afro-Asiatic" is said to include the following linguistic groups or families:

(a) *Semitic languages: Akkadian* (Assyrian, or North Akkadian, Babylonian or South Akkadian) attested in the times of Sargon of Agade around 2350 BC; *Ugaritic* (14th - 13th centuries BC); *Canaanitic* in the first millenium including: *Phoenician* (and its variant *Punic), Hebrew, Ammonitic, Moabitic, Edomitic; Aramaic: ancient Aramaic* (around the 9th - 8th centuries BC), *imperial Aramaic* (around 7th - 4th centuries) and *recent Aramaic* including *Palestinian, Nabatean, Palmyrenian, Hatrean,* then, *Syriaic, Babylonian Aramaic, Mandean,* etc.; Northern Arabic dialects: Lihyanitic, Thamudean, Safaitic, Dedanitic , and Southern Arabian dialects: Minean, Sabaean, Himyaritic, Qatabanic, Hadramutic, Ethiopic (Ge'ez, Amharic). The ancient periods of these Arabic dialects are situated around 600 BC to 600 AD.

(b) The Egyptian language: Ancient Egyptian, Middle Egyptian or Classical Egyptian, neo-Egyptian, Demotic, Coptic. With the Coptic being spoken in Upper Egypt until the 17th century, the spoken Egyptian language lasted about 5000 years, since the oldest texts in hieroglyphs date back to around 3000 BC, and the most recent to the year 394. Coptic has nine main dialectal variants: *Sahidic* (S), *Boharic* (B), *Bachoumouric* (G), *Fayumic* (F) *Achmouninic* (H), *Akhmimic* (A), etc.

(c) The Berber language: from the oasis of Siwa, there is the language of Ghadames, dialects of the central region, such as *Mzabit, Tuareg, Djebel Nefoussa;* the language of the Kabyle, dialects of the Moroccan Rif like those of the *Guelâ'ia*, of the Kibdana, of the Beni Ouriaghel, of the Bot'ioua, the Beni Sa'id and the Temsaman, etc.

It is obvious that *Semitic, Egyptian,* and *Berber* are not genetically linked. The common predialectal ancestor that some want to impose upon these groups of attested languages was *never* reconstructed: "Hamito-Semitic" or "Afro-Asiatic" is only a fantasy, not a linguistic reconstruction (such as Indo-European or Common Semitic) from facts of attested languages.

"Hamito-Semitic" or "Afro-Asiatic" is only a simple scientific hoax which unfortunately still persists, since E. Hincks (1842) and T. Benfey (1844). Marcel Cohen (1947) and J.H. Greenberg (1952) persisted with this scientific hoax. The "*Afro-Asiatic*" journal edited by Robert Hetzron (Santa Barbara, California, USA) and Russell G. Schuh (Los Angeles, California, USA) is one more hoax: the studies published by this journal are more detailed studies connected with such or such particular ·linguistic systems (Hebrew, Arabic, Egyptian, Amharic, etc.), *but never with comparative studies* (Hebrew-Egyptian-Akkadian-

Ethiopian, etc.).

"Hamito-Semitic" or "Afro-Asiatic" reminds us of another famous scientific swindle, but this time in archaeology, the bogus discovery of the alleged remains of prehistoric man, *Piltdown Man* in 1912.

What is in the truth, the reality of Hamito-Semitic or Afro-Asiatic when we consider the following facts?

Akkadian : *sămaš, shamash,* "sun"	Ancient Egyptian: r^c, *râ*
	Coptic : *rē, rě, rěi, ri*
Berber : *tafukt*	
Ugaritic : *špš*	
Hebrew : *šemeš*	

Common Semitic + *šmš*. The Arabic language is truly Semitic: *šams,* "sun".

Can one find a common original form to all these historically attested forms on a visibly inherited lexeme? No linguistic reasoning allows us to do so. "Hamito-Semitic" or "Afro-Asiatic" which would be this common predialectal form does not exist in the materiality of facts.

Elsewhere, this same inherited word "sun" obviously unites Indo-European languages:

Sanskrit	: *súra-, súrya*
Gothic	: *sauil,* and its derivative *sunno*
Latin	: *sōl*
German	: *sonne*
English	: *sun*
Greek	: *hēlios,* Aeolian *āélios,* Cretan *abélios,* Dorian *ālios,* Arcadian *aélios,* with or

                   without aspirate
Welsh   : *haul*
Lithuanian   : *sáulē* (feminine derivative)

All these historical forms allow us to put a radical with a remarkable vocalism: + *sāwel* -, + *sūl*, "sun", in reconstructed, predialectal Indo-European.

Egyptian rather belongs to Black African to form an evident linguistic family.

Ancient Egyptian	: r^c, *ra*, "sun"		
Coptic	: *rē, rĕ, rĕi, ri*		
Sidamo (Kushitic)	: *arrĭšō*		
Saho-Afa (Kushitic)	: *ayrō*		
Rendille (Kenya)	: *orr'ah*, "sun"		
Songhay (Niger)	: *ra*	Numu: *re*	
Vai (Liberia)	: *ra*	Huela: *re*	
Susu (Guinea)	: *ra*	Ligbi : *re*	
Gbin	: *ra*		Samo : *re*
Kono	: *ra*		

We also have this inherited word: "earth, country, region":

Akkadian	: *erṣetu*	Ancient Egyptian: *t3, ta*	
Ugaritic	: *'arṣ*	Coptic	: *tō, to, tĕ*
Hebrew	: *'ereṣ*		
Syriac	: *ar'ā*		
Arabic	: *'ard, 'ardh*		
Berber	: *akal*		

Here again, where is the reality of "Hamito-Semitic" or "Afro-Asiatic", which is supposed to be the common form of all these attested historical forms?

As expected, Egyptian is obviously Black African:

Ancient Egyptian: *t3, ta,* "earth, country, region"
Coptic	: *tō, to, tĕ-*
Nuer (Sudan)	: *thau*
Gmbwaga (Republic of Central Africa)	: *to*
Gbanziri (Republic of Central Africa)	: *to*
Monzombo (Republic of Central Africa)	: *to*
Degema (Nigeria)	: *ù-tò*
Bantu (or proto-Bantu)	: + *sí*

Let us take another inherited word, just as difficult to borrow from another language: the word "mouth": one speaks, eats and drinks with the mouth:

Akkadian	: *pu,* "mouth"	Ancient Egyptian: *r3, ra*	
Ugaritic	: *p*	Coptic	: *ra, rō, ro, rĕ, la, lō, lĕ*
Hebrew	: *pē*	Berber	: *imi*
Phoenician	: *p*	Ghadamsi	: *ami*
Arabic	: *fam, pl. afmām*	Zenaga	: *immi*
		Ethiopian	: *'af*

That it is difficult to contemplate and dare put a *common radical* to all these Semitic, Egyptian and Berber forms, is obvious. It is only necessary to open one's eyes.

On the contrary, Pharaonic Egyptian and Coptic are well and truly Black African in this broad context:

Ancient Egyptian	: *r3, ra,* "mouth"
Coptic	: *ra, rō, ro, rĕ, la, lō, lĕ*
Isekiri (Nigeria)	: *arũ*
Bozo	: *lo*
Kpele	: *la*
Sarakolle (Mali)	: *la*
Busa	: *le*
Guro (Ivory Coast)	: *le*
Ndemli (Benue - Congo)	: *lu*

A name is a universal cultural phenomenon: it identifies the one who carries it, and so differentiates one from other individuals. Also on this point, there is no cultural, linguistic "Haimito-Semitic" or "Afro-Asiatic" universe:

Akkadian	: *šumu, shumu,* "name"	Ancient Egyptian: *rn*
Ugaritic	: *šēm, shēm*	Coptic : *ran, rĕn, lan, lĕn, rin*
Hebrew	: *šēm, shēm*	
Aramaic	: *šum, shum*	
Ethiopian	: *sôm*	
Arabic	: *'ism*	

The palatoalveolar fricative consonant of Akkadian, Ugaritic, Hebrew, and Aramaic, disappears in Arabic and Ethiopian. Berber is: *ism, isem,* "name".

It is virtually impossible to find a common predialectal form to Semitic and Egyptian languages on these terms, which can only be inherited. Therefore, where is the reality, when it comes to verifiable facts, of the "Hamito-Semitic" family or "Afro-

Asiatic" family?

On the other hand, the Egyptian language, obviously connects with other black African languages:

Ancient Egyptian	: *rn*, "name"
Coptic	: *ran, rĕn, lan, lĕn, rin*
Shilluk (Sudan)	: *rin*
Galke (Adamawa)	: *rìn*
Pormi (Adamawa)	: *rìn*
Ngoumi	: *rìn*
Pandjama	: *rìn*
Mbe	: *lén*
Bantu	: *rína, lína, dína, ína, jína, zína*
Fanti (Ghana)	: *dzin*
Asante (Ashanti)	: *din'*

Even if relations are often obscure between the following words, they are nevertheless related and refer to the fact of a common origin:

Latin	: *nōmen*, "name"
Sanskrit	: *nāma*
Avestic	: *nāma*
Gotic	: *namo*
Hittite	: *lāman* (without doubt issued from a dissimulation)
Welsh	: *enw*
Old Irish	: *ainm*
Old Slav	: *imę*
Old Prussian	: *emmens*
Albanian	: *emër, êmen*
Armenian	: *anun*

Tokharian A	: *ñom*; Tokharian.B: *ñem*
Greek	: *hónoma, hoúnoma* (Homeric),
	hónuma in Dorian (*h* = aspirated)
	Radical: + *nõmn*

The families are also distinct:

Semitic	: *sumum, samum, shumu, shĕm,*
	shum, etc.
Indo-European	: *nōmen, nom, name, nama,* etc.
Afro-Egyptian	: *rn, ran, rĕn, lĕn, rin, rina,* etc.

Where is the "Hamito-Semitic" or "Afro-Asiatic" in the above mentioned examples? One can confirm that the "Afro-Asiatic" family is evidently a scientific hoax. One must consequently rid African linguistics of this fake family, which does not exist in the materiality of verifiable facts.

For the word "house", we have:

Hebrew	: *bayit,* "house" (as opposed to "tent":
	ōhel)
South Arabic	: *byt,* pl. *'byt*
Arabic	: *bayt*
Berber	: *tigemmi,* "house" (or *akhkham*).
Ancient Egyptian	: *pr,* "house"
Coptic	: *pĕr-*

The other modern Black African languages, say:

Wolof	: *per,* "fence of the house", "house"
	by extension
Loko	: *pèrè,* "house"

Mende	: *pèrè,*
Kpele	: *pèrè,*
Loma (Toma)	: *pèlè,* (p-r/p-l)
Mofu	: *ver* (*p-r/v-r*)
Uzam	: *ver*
Zidim	: *ver*

Finally, where is the pertinence of the "Hamito-Semitic" or "Afro-Asiatic", with this group of words which is only used in the imperative?:

Akkadian	: *sabat,* "take"
Arabic	: *hud, hudh,* "take", "hold"
Ethiopian	: *yāz*
Berber	: *amez̦*
Ancient Egyptian	: *mi*
Coptic	: *mo, ma*

Once more, the Egyptian language belongs to the whole family of black African languages:

Ancient Egyptian	: *mi,* "take"
Coptic	: *mo, ma*
Yoruba	: *mú*
Banda (Central African: *mi* Republic)	
Mbochi (Bantu)	: *má*
Fang (Gabon)	: *mē*

See the word "black":

Arabic	: 'aswad, "black"
Berber	: *istif, dlu, bekhkhen*
Ancient Egyptian	: *km*

Coptic   : *kame, kĕmi, kam, kĕm*

The Egyptian connects with the black African:

Ancient Egyptian	: *km,* "black" (from *km.t,* "Black
	land", "Black country" = "Egypt")
Coptic	: *kame, kĕmi, kam, kĕm,* "black"
Mbochi (Congo)	: *i- káma,* "coalman", "darkness"
Bambara (Mali)	: *kami,* "to reduce to embers"
	(*km,* "pile of burning wood" in
	Pharaonic)
Mossi (Burkina Faso): *kim,* "to burn"	
Vai (Liberia)	: *kembu,* "charcoal"
Yaaku	: *-kumpu-,* "black"

So, with words like "black", "take" (which is in fact a whole phrase), "house", "name", "mouth", "earth", "country", "region", "sun" and so many others, it is proved radically impossible (strictly in historical linguistics terms, which are comparative and inductive) to find common roots between Semitic languages: Akkadian, Agaritic, Hebrew, Arabic, Ethiopian, etc.; the Egyptian language: Ancient Pharaonic Egyptian, Demotic, Coptic; and the Berber dialects: Siwa, Ghadames, Riffian, Tuareg, Kabyle, etc. Such possible common roots would be a reconstruction which could be validly called "Afro-Asiatic" or "Hamito-Semitic", that is to say, a linguistic family which would unite some African-Berber languages, Egyptian, Ethiopian and the languages of Asia and the Middle East (Akkadian, Hebrew, Arabic, Phoenician, etc.) under one group. Well, it is absolutely impossible to reconstruct such original roots from inherited words.

So, all things well considered, the "Hamito-Semitic" or "Afro-Asiatic" family does not exist in the materiality of facts. Those who want to impose this unreal linguistic family at all cost, manifestly commit an intellectual swindle.

But what,finally, is the significance of all of this? One can only interpret this as that the champions of "Afro-Asiatic" want "to play" and "to cheat" with history:

1. They want to put the ancient world of the Jewish people (the Hebrews) and the Pharaonic world of the Nile Valley on an equal footing, although we know that the Hebrews created no significant contribution to the development of civilization in antiquity except in religion for which Ancient Egypt is owed a tremendous debt.

2. Above all, they want to cut the Pharaonic world from the black African cultural universe, by wrongly preaching, obviously, that the language which supports the Pharaonic civilization has nothing in common with the languages spoken today by black Africans. Therefore, logically, the Pharaonic cultural and linguistic world does not belong to the black African world on the whole.

The Afro-Asiatic is a mere myth that must be destroyed.

6. Some morphological correspondences between Egyptian and black African

We have completed a rather detailed work regarding all the fundamental aspects of the common grammatical and formal structures between Ancient Egypt and Black Africa. Here, we would only like to emphasise a few unarguable and precise facts.

There is a most remarkable correlation, a perfect concordance between the third person singular of the Egyptian and the Wolof suffix *pronoun*, both masculine and feminine: Ancient Egyptian *.f, .s,* Wolof *.ef, .es;* for the third person plural, the Wolof is closer to Pharaonic Egyptian than Coptic itself: Ancient Egyptian *sn*, Coptic *ou*, Wolof, *sen:*

Ancient Egyptian: *mr. n. f,* "he loved"
                   mr. n. s, "she loved"
                   mr. n. sn, "they loved"
Wolof   : *mār. an. ef,* "he loved madly"
                   mār. on. es, "she loved madly"
                   mār. on. sen, "they love madly"
                   (they also say: *mar. on. nanw*)

This concordance concerns a specific point, peculiar to Egyptian and Wolof morphology. Let us note what follows:

Ancient Egyptian: *mr,* "to love" "to desire"; *mrw. t,*
                   "love"
Coptic   : *mĕrĕ, mĕri, mĕlli, mĕ, mĕri,*

	maĕriĕ, mi, id.
Acoli (Nilotic)	: *maaro,* "to love", *maar,* "love"
Lwo, Luo (Nilotic)	: *mer,* "to agree, to be in accord with", "kindness"
Nuer (Nilotic)	: *mar,* "friend"
Mangbetu (North-East Zaire)	: *o-mu, omu,* "to love"; *mu,* "friend"
Wolof (Atlantic)	: *mār,* "to love madly"
Hebrew (by comparison)	: *ahab,* "love"
Arabic (by comparison)	: *habba,* "to love" "to desire"; *'ahabba,* "to be fond of, to love"; *hubb,* "love, affection, attachment"

Furthermore, the Coptic (which is Ancient Egyptian vocalised) and the Bambara (Mali) present similar verbal forms:

Coptic
i' na'di, "I will give"
n na-di, "we will give"
oŭ na-di, "he/she will give"

Bambara (West Africa):
i nā-di, "you will give"
an nā-di, "they will give"
oŭ nā-di, "he/she will give"

The functional element *n* in Egyptian, Coptic *na,* Bambara *na,* Wolof *on,* expressly indicates the future. One finds the same functional *na* everywhere in the field of black Africa. For example, in Luganda (Uganda):

Bambara (West Africa)
n' nā-be, "I will be"

Luganda (African Great Lakes)
n-naa-ba, "I will be" (*ba,* "to be"

i nā-be, "you will be"   *o naa-ba,* "you will be"
a nā-be, "he/she will be"   *a-naa-ba,* "he/she will be"

There is another Pharaonic particle to explicitly indicate the future: *ka* and the form *sedjem.ka.ef,* "to hear", which are mostly encountered in religious texts and inscriptions in temples: *hâ. ka. sen. ma. sen tou,* "They will certainly rejoice when they see you" (*Urk.* IV, 569 10); *peri. ka Hâpi er pet,* "Hapi (the flood of the Nile) will rise to the sky".

In Hausa, we have *ka,* whose use is above all confined to the poetic (Charles H. Robinson, *Hausa Grammar,* p.36). In Baguirmien, the particle *ka* is also present to indicate the future: *i mala ka tad,* "you will make yourself" (*i,* "you"; *tad/a,* "to do"); *ne ka tad,* "he will do" (*ne,* "he, him").

In Fang, the immediate and distant future is expressed with the element *ke* : *me ke so akiri,* "I am coming tomorrow" (*me,* "I, me"; *so,* "to come", "to arrive"; *akiri,* "tomorrow", *kiri,* "morning").

In Kimbundu, it is the particle *ka* which is used to form the distant future: *eme nga ka landa,* "I will do the shopping" (*landa,* "to buy, to do the shopping"). In Bambara, after the verb *be,* "to be", the particle *ka* is used to translate various tenses of the verb, among which is the future: *min bi ka nin ke,* "the one who will do this" (*min,* "the one who"; *nin* "this is, that is, this"; *ke,* "to do"). In Mbochi, the particle *ka* explicitly indicates the future: *bà ka badzwà pòò,* "they will go to the village" (*bà,* "they, them"; *idzwà,* "to go", "to leave"; *pòò,* "village"). In Mancagne, the constructions which indicate the future are: *bia ka, lun ka, ia ka*. For the immediate future, one uses the construction *ia ka*: *a ia ka lilendar*, "he will rejoice".

How could Hausa borrow the *ka* from Kimbundu or Mbochi? How could Bambara borrow the *ka* from Ancient Egyptian? How could Fang borrow the *ke* from Baguirmain? According to the method in operation, there is a link of origin:

Ancient Egyptian *ka*
Hausa (Nigeria) *ka*
Baguirmien (Chad) *ka*
Fang (Gabon) *ke*
Mbochi (Congo) *ka*
Kimbundu (Angola) *ka*
Bambara (Mali) *ka*
Mancagne *ia ka*
(Ziguinchor, South Senegal and Guinea-Bissau)

In Ancient Egyptian, there is only one way of translating the *negative imperative*: we use *m*, from the verb *imi*, itself a negative verb (Gardiner, *Egyptian Grammar*, § 340, § 345).

Here are some examples: *ir*, "do", *m ir* "don't" (to a close friend); *snd*, "be afraid", m snd, "don't be afraid"; *m rdi kt m st kt*, "do not substitute this for that other" (*Urk.* IV 1090, 9; 1091. 2).

This negative imperative of Pharaonic Egyptian *m* is a singular, pertinent fact, almost idiomatic. In Yoruba, the negative form *ma* is also used to grammatically form the negative imperative: 'The negative of the simple form of command is formed by placing the particle *ma* before the verb' (E. L. Lasebikan, *Learning Yoruba*, Oxford University Press, 1958, p.58).

In Pharaonic Egyptian as in Yoruba, *m/má* is a particle employed *solely* and *exclusively* for the negative imperative. Pharaonic Egyptian: *m ir,* "don't"; Yoruba *joko,* "sit down"; *má joko,* "don't sit". In Arabic: *'if ᶜal,* "do"; *la taf ᶜal,* "don't"; *hud,* "take"; *la tahud,* "don't take". The element *la* is the negative. This is a typical, singular, pertinent encounter for it is the same phonetic reality (*m'má*), same morphology, same syntax (its use strictly limited to the negative imperative, the same initial position). It is therefore a consequence of total concordance: lexicologic, morphologic, syntactic, phonetic, between Pharaonic Egyptian and Yoruba.

The *liaison particles* are grammatical significations which establish specific relations. To speak like Ferdinand de Saussure, liaison particles express a host of connections in so far as grammatical and lexicological means. Liaison particles (conjunctions, prepositions, etc.) are invariable words which link juxtaposed elements in a sentence; they bring a nuance or precision of meaning, and also work in relation to an ensemble of other elements linked between them, to express syntactical, grammatical relations. Usually, the liaison particle is a consonant followed by a vowel.

The psychological, grammatical mechanism relation in Pharaonic Egyptian and in Coptic is done with the same linguistic tools, the same signification and particles as in the mechanisms of modern Black African languages. Here are some examples:

1.

Ancient Egyptian	: *m,* "within, out of, with, by means of, like, as much as, in, when, while, then"
Coptic	: `*m-,* `*mmo,* "inside, during, of, out of, by means of"; `*m pai- ma,* "in these premises, within this place," `*n-t-sẽfi,* "by the word," "by means of the sword" (*m* turns into *n* before *t*)
Acoli (Nilotic)	: *me,* "the, for, of"
Banda (Central African Republic)	: *ma, me,* "inside, to, at"
Ngbandi (Central African Republic)	: *ma,* "like"
Luganda (Uganda)	: *mu,* "inside"
Sena (Zambia)	: *mu,* "when"
Soubiya (Zambia)	: *m, mo, umo,* "there" (Pharaonic Egyptian *m, im,* "there")
Zulu (South Africa)	: *ma, uma* "when"
Ronga (Mozambique)	: *mo, mu,* "inside"
Baoule (Ivory Coast)	: *mo,* "inside" (with, above all, the names of village, of the country).
Senufo (Manianka, Mali)	: *ma/na,* "for, in favour of, at",
Hausa (Nigeria)	: *ma,* "at, for" (*ma ka,* "yours")
Bambara (Mali)	: *ma,* "when/as, like"
Berber (for comparison)	: *d'i, d'eg,* "at, inside, in"; *d', id',* "with (*ifal Essoudan*

		did terekfin, "He went to the Sudan by caravan", Ghadamès. Again we have in Berber: *r'ef,* "because of"; *g,* "inside"; *s, sa,* "when"; *akken,* "when/as"; *dus, dous, doussen,* "there"
Arabic (for comparison)	:	*fi,* "in": *fi al-bayt,* "in the house" when Pharaonic Egyptian is : *m pr,* "inside the house" (*m,* "inside").
II. Ancient Egyptian	:	*r,* "around, subject to, friendly with, against, for"
Coptic	:	*ĕ-, ĕro,* "at, towards, of, outside, on"; *ero. f,* "at his"; *ĕ p- schafĕ,* "about the desert, at the desert"
Bambara (Mali)	:	*ra, ro,* "at, of"
Mangbetu (East Zaire)	:	*ru,* "with, by means of"
Nuer (Nilotic)	:	*re,* "between"
Songhay (Niger)	:	*ra,* "in, inside, inside of"
Azer (Medieval Soninke)	:	*ra, re,* "at"
Arabic (for comparison)	:	*ilā,* "about, at": *ilā sahrā'.* "about the desert".
III. Ancient Egyptian	:	*n,* "for, at, because of, of" (dative and genetive)
Coptic	:	`n-, `n=, "at" (dative): *pĕdjō.oŭ na.f,* "they will tell him" (*na,* "at"; *na.f,* "to him"); *n* becomes *m* before *p:* `m-pi-kosmos, "at the world"

Baguirmien	:	*an.* "for, at, of"
Hausa	:	*na,*"of": *dokin Dauda = doki na Dauda,*"David's horse"
Senufo	:	*ni,* "at, of"
Bambara	:	*na,* "at"
Tsogho (South Gabon)	:	*na,* "at, because of"
Mpongwe (Coastal Gabon)	:	*ni, na,* "for, because of, by,in"
Ngabndi (Zaire)	:	*na,* "at"
Gourmantché (Burkina Faso)	:	*n,* "relating to, with"
Lingala (Zaire, Congo)	:	*na,* "of, at": *ndako na biso,* "our house (literally: "*house of ours*"); *na,* "by, for": *na bolingo,* "by love, because of love"
Berber (for comparison)	:	*i, d, et,* "at, for, because of love"

The concordance of the three Egyptian particles: *m, r* and *n* (Coptic, `*m-, `*mmo; ĕ-, ĕro; `*n-, `*n=, na*) with the corresponding ones in modern black African languages confirm, if still necessary, the profound ties of origin between Pharaonic Egyptian, Coptic and Black African. Facts are facts. It is not permitted to cheat with the facts. A profound, formal and grammatical link exists between Egyptian and Black African. It is the only legitimate conclusion to draw from facts such as the ones just delineated.

7. Examples of phonetic correspondence between the Egyptian and the Black African

Clearly and simply, this question is one of internal and reductive analysis, which one has to bring in formulating phonetic laws. From then on, phonetic analysis is the most essential and instructive part of the comparison. It is a question of establishing rules of phonetic correspondences between the compared languages.

Phonetic alteration, change, and linguistic transformations are not isolated incidents. They occur quite regularly and are determined in all cases where the same conditions are realised. Example: The Latin /p/ of *saponem* remains in the Italian *sapone,* but changes slightly in the provençal *sabo,* and even more, in becoming an aspirant in the French *savon;* it is the same for the Latin *ripam* which becomes *riba* in provençal and *rive* in French. We have here a phonetic /p/ > /b/ > /v/, in the series examined.

Sometimes, the differences which are not apparent can baffle the uninitiated: *florem* gives *fleur* (flower), *cantatorem* gives *chanteur* (singer). How can one explain the transformations? It is rather simple, the Latin *o* stressed in open syllable, leads to the French *eu.*

There is a systematic correspondence between the English /d/ and the German /t/: English *drink* / German *trinken;* English *door* / German *tür;* English *dream* / German *traum.*

But it is required not to reason from borrowed words: the Serbo-Croatian words *avlija*, "court";

pendžer, "window"; *dimnije,* "women's clothing"; *kilim,* "carpet", etc., are Turkish words, and history tells us that the Turks colonised the Slavs-Yugoslavians (the Slavs of the South) for almost three and a half centuries. From then on, Serbo-Croatian is not under the influence of the dominant Turkish.

Consequently, one must be able to distinguish the borrowed words owed to geographical contacts and to the history of heritage which comes from the common original language.

The similarities between the *Ewe* and the *Mbochi* (Congo) are truly striking:

Ewe (Togo-Ghana, West Africa)	Mbochi (Congo, Central Africa)
abɔ, "arm"	*ɛ.bo* , arm (open o)
kú, dead	*le.kú, i.kú,* "the dead"
ku, "character", "conduct"	*e.kú,* "jealousy"
me, "to burn"	*miá,* "fire"
mi, "to swallow"	*i. miǎ,* "to swallow"
ta, "saliva"	*a.tɛ* "saliva"
te, "stand up"	*tɛɛ,* "stand up"
to, "to grow, to shoot, to produce"	*tɔɔ,* "to germinate, to grow"
tó ,"family, parent"	*i. tɔ,* "to marry"

Chance cannot explain such facts, even less the borrowing of words. It can only be due to a remote, prehistorical link.

When we have a series with the initial /d/ like with the word "to eat", it can only be inherited:

Mancagne	: *dɛ* ,"to eat"
Mossi	: *di*
Gourmantche	: *di/dye*
Senoufo	: *di*
Ewe	: *du*
Kikongo	: *-dia/-dya*
Kuba	:*o-dia, -dia*
Shilele	: *ku-dia, -dia*

Lunda	: *ku-de, -de*
Mbochi	: *i-dza, dza*
Yoruba	: *jẹ, djɛ*

That is to say, a series which cover Africa from Guinea-Bissau (Mancagne) in Central Africa (Luba, Lunda, etc.) to different geographical locations on the continent, it is difficult or nearly impossible to put down to chance such examples of obvious phonetic connections.

On the contrary, these series reveal a profound link with the relevant languages: these relatively recent, though different pronunciations, (*di, dia, du, de, djè dza*, etc.) imply a unique, more ancient pronunciation, as in the French *nuit*, Spanish *noche*, Italian *notte*, recent forms linked to a more ancient ($\pm$ *nocte*).

We have in Pharaonic Egyptian d^c = *djâ*, which means: "spices for bread" (*Urk.* IV, 1157, 15). And the Coptic: *djē*, "a dish". A comparatist notes first that on the semantic level, there is a slight evolution: *bread, a dish for nourishment, to eat*, are realities which capture the same field of signification, and recall a daily reality (bread, dish, to eat).

But the really important point is that we have the same word which hardly developed phonetically (Ancient Egyptian *dyâ*, Mbochi *-dza*, Teke *dza*, Fang *zi, dzi*; Coptic *djē*, Yoruba *djè djɛ, je*) and the phoenetic mutations are almost self-explanatory: Baoule *li*, "to eat"; Vili *ku-lia, -lia*; Mbe *ò-lía/líe: dia/lia; di/li.*

We can therefore affirm that all these forms: *djâ, djē, dza, dia, di, de, du, dye, lia, dzi, zi, za*, etc., refer to the same and only ancestral phonetic form. In other words, ancient Pharaonic Egyptian, Coptic and modern Black African languages are genetically and historically linked.

Berber is not linked with this African Egyptian family: Berber *etch*, "to eat", aortic *itchou*.

The Akan (Ghana) is evidently Black African: *didi*, "to eat" in Asante (Ashanti), and *dzidzi*, "to eat" in Fanti: the Akan has simply doubled the simple form (*di/didi; dzi/dzidzi*).

In Arabic we have: *akala*, "to eat", and *'akl*, "food". This is manifestly different from the forms: *djâ, dza, dzi, djē, di, de, dia, lia, li*, etc., from Black African languages, since Pharaonic Egyptian.

After these remarks and general observations, we can analyse in a much deeper way the phonetic correspondences on one or two precise examples, for there is no space for more ample demonstrations, which are quite tedious for those who are not specialists in comparative linguistics.

The muffled dorso-velar occlusive /k/

The initial and mid-vowel: the same position and frame in Ancient Egyptian, in Coptic and in Mbochi (Congo, Bantu language). Therefore:

-/k/ Introduces a bilabial nasal occlusive /m/:

Pharaonic Egyptian: *km,* "black"
Coptic   : k̲amĕ, k̲am, k̲ĕmi, k̲ĕm,"black"
(evolved Egyptian)
Mbochi (Bantu)   : *i-kama,* "to mine for coal, to
                      blacken".

Therefore, we have these phonetic alterations at consonant level: *k- k- k-* and *-m -m -m.* The consonantal structure is not rigorously the same everywhere. The *a* of Coptic *kamĕ, kam,* recurs in Mbochi: *i-kama,* the *i* — being a prefix of the infinitive, and the final *a* of *i -kama* being only a supportive vowel. Therefore, Coptic and Mbochi are absolutely identical phonetically.

/ k / Introduces another muffled dorso-velar occlusive / k /

Pharaonic Egyptian: k̲kw, "darkness"
Coptic   : k̲alĕ, k̲ĕkĕ, "darkness"
Mbochi   : ε.kɔkɔ, "evening darkness"

This gives these phoenetic correspondences: k̲- k̲- k̲- and -k̲ -k̲ -k̲. The three lexemes, in fact, rest upon an identical consonantal base: = $k^w k^w$ "darkness" of the evening, of the night (the ancient Egyptian word being written with a determinative which perfectly allows it to speak of darkness of evening, darkness, or nocturnal darkness).

-/k/ Introduces two muffled dental occlusives/tt/:

Pharaonic Egyptian: k̲tt, "small"
Coptic   : k̲oy, koyĕ, "small"
Mbochi   : k̲yɛ̀, "small, little".

In Coptic and Mbochi, these two consonants /tt/ have disappeared. This phenomenon is very constant in Coptic Egyptian. But this disappearance led to a diphtongization, and the Mbochi again presents: ɛ.kɛ̀ɛ̀, "small, little". The Kikongo offers: *nke, -ke,* "small, little". On the other hand, the muffled dental is still there in Sango (Central African Republic): *kɛtɛ,* "small, little": *lo mu na mbi ingo kɛtɛ,* "he has given me a little salt" (literally: "he gave to me little salt").

-/k/ is introduced by a deaf /s/:

Pharaonic Egyptian : *sk₃, ska,* "to plough" (not a
                         causative)
Coptic   : *sĕk̲ai, sĕk̲ayi,* "to plough"
Mbochi   : *i-sàk̲à* (dialectal variant: *i-*
                         sàà) "to plough"
Kikongo   : *ku-sààkà,* "to harvest, to reap
                         cereals, to hoe".

We therefore have : s̲- s̲- s̲- and -k̲ -k̲ -k̲

So, for the facts examined here, the phonetic correspondences are absolutely rigorous between Pharaonic Egyptian, Coptic and Mbochi, notably at consonantal level, the very frame of the words.

The apico-alveolar vibrant /r/

This phoneme is very interesting to analyse.

Pharaonic Egyptian: *rmt,* "man", "to be human"
Coptic   : *rōmĕ,* "man", "husband"
                    rōmi
                    ōmi

The apico-alveolar vibrant of Pharaonic Egyptian loses its vibration and becomes an apico-alveolar lateral in Coptic, in the Fayumic dialect: *rmt/lōmi* (*r/l*).   In the Bantu-Mbochi language of the Congo, there is also an *i* which presents itself as: *o-lómì,* "husband, spouse", "male".

So, we have three series with /r/, with /l/ and with a zero series — without an initial consonant for the words: "man, husband, spouse":

(a) Series with /r/:

Pharaonic Egyptian: *rmt*
Coptic   : *rōmĕ, rōmi*
Nuer (Sudan)   : *răm,* "human person, individual"
Azer (Mali)   : *reme, remme,* "child" (semantic transfer)

(b) Series with : /l/

Coptic   : *lōmi*
Azer   : *leme, lemme*

Common Bantu   : + *-lúmi*
Mbochi   : *o-lómì*, pl. *a-lómì*
Topoke (Zaire)   : *-lome*
Luba (Kasai, Zaire) : *mu-lume*
Teke (Tio, Congo)   : *o-lúm', n-lum', mu-lum'*

(c) **Series with /n/** :

Fang (Gabon)   : *n-nôm*
Mponwe (Gabon) : *o-nome, o-nomo*
Kuba (Zaire)   : *num, nuum*
Vili (Congo)   : *nunni* (attraction of *m* which
                       becomes *n*)

(e) **Zero series**

Tetela (Zaire)   : *oṁi* (facing *rōmĕ/lōmi;
                       lumi/nôm/num/lum*)
Lomongo (Zaire)   : *b-ome* (*b* - nominal prefix)
Ntomba (Zaire)   : *bo-ome* (*bo-* class prefix)
Tsogho (Gabon)   : *m-ome*, pl. *a-ome*
Akwa Opa   : *mo-omi*, pl. *b- ami.*

We notice that the /r/ underwent modifications: *r/r* (maintaining), but *r/l* and *r/l/n* were permuted. However, the nasal bilabial /m/ appears everywhere as the nucleus-consonant, the fundamental element, without change: *rmt, rōmĕ, rōmi, răm, reme, lōmi, leme, lume, lumi ,o-lomi, mu-lume, n-nôm, o-nome* (*o-rome/o-lome/-o-nome,*), *num* (*o-nume/o-rome/o-lome*), *omi, -ome, omi* (*rōmĕ/lome/nome /ome*). This clearly speaks of a family relation, which permits us to clearly see the history of the compared languages, their characteristic innovations in relation to more ancient forms (Pharaonic Egyptian, Coptic).

The phonetic rule is as follows: The Egyptian /r/ (Pharaonic and Coptic), in losing its vibration, became a lateral in the Fayumic Coptic dialect /l/.   This lateral, becoming more nasal, became an apicodental nasal occlusive /n/.   So: *r̠mt* /*rōmě*, *r̠ōmi/lōmi/o-lomi/nome.* In the same way: "mouth" in Pharaonic, *r̠ɜ, ra,* in Coptic *rō, la, lō,* and in Mbochi *ɔ.n ɔ̀ɔ̀* , "mouth"; Fongbe *nu, nû;* Yoruba *ẹnu,* Ewe *nu,* Fanti *anu,* Baoulé *ne,* Bini (Edo) *unu,* Mossi *no;* Bozo *lo,* Sarakolle *la,* etc.

8. **A few lexicological correspondences**

The resemblance of the words examined here can be explained by an identity of origin, for these resemblances, both in form and meaning, convey terms, manifestly inherited: the compared languages have not been in contact recently, except for the contacts of origin, before the division of the languages. On the other hand, the testimony of two or three non-adjacent languages, remote in space, favours the original link, since chance is excluded on inherited terms. Therefore:

1. Pharaonic Egyptian   : *bâi,* "palm"
   Coptic   : *ba, bae, bai, bei,*
                            palm", "palm branch"
   Mbochi (Congo)   : *i-bía,* "palm tree"
   Teke   : *bá,* "palm tree"
   (Congo, Gabon, Zaire)
   Lokonda (Zaire)   : *i-bá,* "palm tree"
   Mofu (North Cameroon) : *tu-bah*
   Arabic (for comparison) : *nahla,* "palm", "palm

tree", "date palm"

2. Pharaonic Egyptian   : *ba,* "spirit, soul"

   Coptic   : *bai,* "spirit, soul"
   Mbochi (Congo)   : *bà,* "to be sound in
                               spirit", "to be spiritually
                               honest"
   Ronga (Mozambique)   : *ku-ba, -ba,* "to be"
                               (the *b* is a fricative)
   Songhay (Niger)   : *bi* (*bi-yo*), "double of a
                               being", "soul"
   Mangbetu   : *o-bu,* "to be, to
   (North-East Zaire)   exist" (to have spirit)
   Bambara (Mali)   : *be, bi,* "to be, to exist"
                               (to have spirit)
   Arabic (for comparison)   : *ñafs,* "soul". "essence",
                               "being"
                               ruh, "vital breath"

3. Pharaonic Egyptian   : *bin,* "bad"
   Coptic   : *boonĕ, baanĕ, boni,
                               bani,* "bad"
   Mbochi (Congo)   : *e-béná,* "infirmed", "ill"
   Wolof (Senegal)   : *bōn,* "bad"
   Bambara (Mali)   : *bone,* "bad luck"
   Azer (Medieval Soninke)   : *bane,* "bad"
   Sénoufo   : *buon,* "bad luck"
   Songhay (Niger)   : *bone,* "ill"
   Peul   : *bone,* "maliciousness"
   Mossi   : *bone,* "ill, bad"
   Kaje (Nigeria, Plateau)   : *biyin,* "bad"
   Arabic (for comparison)   : *šar,* "ill"; *sayyi',* "bad"
                               (*sayyi' assu',* "bad
                               character").

4. Pharaonic Egyptian   : *iba, yiba,* "to dance",
                               "dance"
   Wolof (Senegal)   : *yiba,* "to dance"
   Mangbetu   : *eba,* "to dance",
   (North-East Zaire)

Gmbwaga (CAR)	: *be,* "dance"
Gbanziri (CAR)	: *be,* "dance"
Mondzombo (CAR)	: *be,* "dance"
Caffino (Kushitic, Ethiopia)	: *dū-bō,* "dance"; *du-b,* "to dance"
Bambara (Mali)	: *bo,* "drum" (*bo koro,* "dance hall")
Mbochi (Congo)	: *i-bí-na* (core element - *bi-*), "to dance"
Arabic (for comparison)	: *raqs,* "dance"; *raqasa,* "to dance".

5. Pharaonic Egyptian : *mw,* "water"
  Coptic : *mŏŏu, mōu, maŭ, mŏ, mē*

Mbochi (Congo)	: *má*
Lingala (Zaire, Congo)	: *may* (*mai, maī*)
Yoruba (Nigeria)	: *o-mi, omi*
Bini (Edo, Nigeria)	: *a-mē, amē*
Nago (Benin)	: *omi*
Tiv (Nigeria)	: *mà*
Gwara (Nigeria)	: *ímè*
Margi (Nigeria)	: *'imí*
Pelci (Nigeria)	: *mâ*
Arabic (for comparison)	: *ma'* "water"

6. Pharaonic Egyptian : *mw. t,* "mother"
  Coptic : *măău, mă), mŭu, mo*

Mbochi (Congo)	: *máá, móó*
Mossi (Burkina Faso)	: *ma*
Logba	: *ámá*
Baoule (Ivory Coast)	: *ma* (and *né*)
Bambara (Mali)	: *ma* (and *bá*)
Kabi-Benoue	: *ma*
Wandala	: *mu*
Nuer (South Sudan)	: *mur, mŏr, mar, mwŏr* (*r* additive element)
Zelgwa (North Cameroon)	: *mur*
Sotho (Southern Africa)	: *m̀mé*

Arabic : '*umm*, "mother"
(for comparison)

7. Pharaonic Egyptian : *ka*, "so, then"
   Coptic : *kĕ* - "so, self"
   Acoli (Luo, Lwo) : *ka*, "if, then"
   Mangbetu (Zaire) : *ka*, "therefore"
   Kikongo (Congo) : *e-kà*, "if, then"
   Douala (Cameroon) : *kɛ*, "In this case, then, and
       then"
   Bini (Edo, Nigeria) : '*ke,*, "and then"
   Bambara (Mali) : *ko*, "following behind"

8. Pharaonic Egyptian : *s*, "man" (someone); *z* in
       the Ancient Empire
   Coptic : *sa*, "man; husband"
   Gangero (Kushitic) : *a-sa, asa*, "man"
   Kapsiki : *za* (Ancient Empire *z*)
   Koro : *ò-sa*, "husband"
   Logba : *ɔsá*,"husband"
   Tunen : *mò-sa*, pl. *bà-sa*,"man"
   (South Cameroon)   (radical - *sa*)
   Mbochi (Congo) :*o-sí*, pl. *a-sí* "someone from"
   Sango (CAR) : *zo*, "man" (Ancient Empire *z*)
   Ngandi (CAR, Zaire) : *zo*, "man"
   Mangbetu : *ma-si*, "man,
   (North-East Zaire)   husband, male"
   Common Bantu : + -*sí* (*mu-sí, omu-sí,
       o-sí*, etc.), "folk", "lives at"
   Arabic (for comparison) : *rajul*, "man"; *zawj*,
       "husband, spouse"

9. Pharaonic Egyptian : *ii*, "to come", "to arrive"
   Coptic : *ĕi, i, ĕyĕ, iĕ, yĕ, ĕia,
       ĕya, hiĕ*
   Bantu and Benue-Congo: + -*yɨ*, "to come" "to arrive"

Mbochi (Congo)	: *i-yaa*
Kuba (Zaire)	: *i* (like the Coptic *i*)
Ivili (Gabon)	: *ya*
Duala (Cameroon)	: *ya*
Baoule (Ivory Coast)	: *i* (*i dè*, "come here", like the Coptic *i*)
Gouin	: *yô*
Bete (Ivory Coast)	: *yi, i, gi*
Topoke (Zaire, Equator)	: *-y-* (*yô*, "come"; *yei*, "come on"
Bade	: *àyi*, "come"
Janji (Nigeria, Plateau)	: *'àye*, "to come"
Arabic	: *atā, jā'a*, "to come",
(for comparison)	"to arrive"

10. Pharaonic Egyptian	: *rimi, rmi*, "to cry"
Coptic	: *rimě, rimi, limi*
Birri (Nigeria, Plateau)	: *rami*, "to cry"
Acoli	: *reèmò*, "to make
(Luo, Lwo, Kenya)	someone sad" (to make him cry)
Ewondo (Cameroon)	: *n-sɔm*, "who cries loudly"
Mbochi (Congo)	: *i-samí*, "mocking and teasing to the point of tears" (*r-m/s-m*)
Arabic (for comparison)	: *bakā,* "to cry", "to be tearful

Conclusion

The conclusion is obvious:

1. The "Hamito-Semitic" or the "Afro-Asiatic" is only a scientific invention; a predialectal ancestor common to Semitic, to Berber, and to Egyptian lang-

"

uages was never reconstructed following the method of historically compared linguistics, whose aim is, precisely, to link genetically the solicited languages.

2. The numerous morphological, syntactic, phonetic and lexicological concordances that can be clearly established between Pharaonic Egyptian, Coptic and all modern Black-African languages are of an historical genetic order, and it might be scientifically possible to reconstruct the common predialectal ancestor of all these ancient and modern languages.

3. Consequently, if African linguistic studies go round in circles, it is precisely because of the lack of a new and dynamic methodology, and also because of the tenacious preconception which insists on splitting the Egypto-Nubian Valley of the Nile from the rest of the Black African world.

4. It is imperative not to follow the well trodden paths in the field of inherited African linguistics; not to follow a particular linguistic canon (solely descriptive), but to engage in a veritable general, African comparative and scientific linguistics.

5. This fertile path is the same that was laid out, with devotion and science, by our master, Professor CHEIKH ANTA DIOP.

Appendix : Questions

1. Briefly define the essentials of the historical linguistic method and the goal pursued by this method.

2. Can the historical linguistic method be applied to Black-African languages?

3. Which are the criteria that legitimize and validate the comparison of the Egyptian language (Ancient Egyptian, Coptic) and modern Black-African languages?

4. What should be logically included in the so-called "Afro-Asiatic" linguistic family? Through lunguistic reconstruciton, has a common, predialectal ancestor been established between Semitic, Berber and Pharaonic Egyptian languages (Ancient Egyptian, Coptic)?

5. From the analysis of clearly inherited words like: "sun", "soil" (country, region), "mouth", "name", "house", "black" (adjective), "love", "in", "towards", "eat", "bad", "man", "to come, to arrive", "to cry", etc., can one include in the same related linguistic group, the Semitic language, the Berber language and the Egyptian (Ancient Egyptian, Coptic)?

6. Morphological correlations between Pharaonic Egyptian and Black-African: give precise examples.

7. Phonetic correlations between Pharaonic Egyptian and Black-African: give precise examples.

8. Lexicological correlations between Pharaonic Egyptian and Black-African: give precise examples.

9. Black-African linguistics has been hitherto almost solely descriptive. Other than the fact that it constantly goes round and round in circles, Black-African linguistics admittedly separates the Egypto-Nubian Valley from the rest of Black Africa. In this case, can not historical linguistics, so much neglected in Black Africa, renew the studies on African languages?

4

MALE/FEMALE RELATIONS IN ANCIENT EGYPT

---

oday, in the twentieth century, we understand the organization of civilized society as a separation of legislative, judicial, executive, religious and economic powers. This separation "naturally" engenders a hierarchy among the representatives of these different, distinct powers. To this separation and hierarchy, one must add the social stratifications due to economic production and socio-political relationships, resulting from the production and distribution of national resources. Thus, in such hierarchical societies, whether they be slave-owning, feudal, industrial, technological etc., men, invariably assume essential functions and enjoy powers of decision and therefore dominate women. Hence the movements so characteristic of feminist struggles for the emancipation of women.

We are therefore used to analysing social organizations through a European interpretation of history. From Greco-Roman antiquity to this day, Europe has viewed history *only as a terrain of class struggles;* struggles between citizen and non-citizen, slave and master, plebeian and pretorean, serf and lord, bourgeois and noble, aristocrat and king, peasant and city dweller, worker and bourgeois, man and woman.

By force of habit and through education, we apply the same models to the peoples of old Sumer and Mesopotamia, to the societies of imperial China, to the Mayas and Aztecs, North American Indians, Pacific peoples, peoples and societies of Black Africa.

In Black Africa, one speaks readily of "feudal" societies, kinship and clanic systems, granary systems, age groups, secret societies, partrilineal or matrilineal regimes and all sorts of nonsense which do not stand the test of truth. This is a legacy of ethnographic "science". It was the Morgans, the Bachofens, the Levy-Bruhls and their disciples — functionalists, diffusionists, structuralists — who spoke of "primitive society", "elementary kinship structures", "potlach", "tribe", "gift of women", "prelogical mentality", "savage thought", "universal matriarchy", "primitive arts", "savage people", etc.

There is nothing serious in all this. And the gravest mistake would be to describe pharaonic society with the criteria and models laid down by either ethnography or simplistic marxism. To see in the king or Pharaoh in Egyptian society of antiquity, a replica of kings in mediaeval Europe, is to refuse to face facts. Moreover, there was never slavery in Egyptian society at the time of the Pharaohs. In antiquity, Egyptian women were never dominated by Egyptian men. Lastly, there has never been social classes or struggles between social classes in the marxist sense of the word, not during the long history of ancient Egypt. Let us therefore examine the status of women in Ancient Egypt.

1. Equality Between Men and Women

In antiquity, Egypt stood out as the only country to have truly guaranteed women a status equal to that of men. Since the Old Kingdom, this has been attested to beyond all reasonable doubt. All specialists of Egyptian law — Revillout and Paturet in the nineteenth century and recently Theodorides, Allan and Pestman — have confirmed that Egyptian women were juridically equal to men and enjoyed an equal footing as was the case between sons and daughters.

Egyptian women could own or acquire assets, contract or undertake whatever without hindrance. As from birth, Egyptian women enjoyed full rights and *no change* as to their legal status occurred, on account of either their getting married or their bearing children.

2. The Freedom of Women

Egyptian women did not experience the particular

form of tutelage Roman women were subjected to.

The *power of parents* was above all a form of *protection.* In case of succession, the responsibilities for men and women were identical. Egyptian women were relatively free to choose their would-be spouses. Such independence was still strongly evident at the close of the indigenous dynasties to warrant two Greek tragic poets — Sophocles (c. 495 - 406 BC) and Euripides (480 - 406 BC) — to describe, in many of their works, Egyptian men as "sitting in a corner whilst their women folk dealt with all the household affairs". With his famous *Prostagna,* Ptolemy IV, Philapator I, the Greek king of Egypt from between 221 - 203 BC, partly revoked traditional Egyptian law by questioning the notion of equality between the sexes. This could only have been so because of the Greek system of patriarchal control in a setting of matrilineality.

The notion of "caste" does not seem to have existed in Pharaonic Egypt. Indeed all prerogatives were granted to Egyptian women. Like men, Egyptian women were called by their *name,* which, as early as the Middle Kingdom, was preceded — if they were married — by the expression *Nebet-per* meaning "household mistress". However, though the legal status of women was similar to that of men in the Old Kingdom, they were nonetheless compelled to obey a moral imperative, that is, to be virgins before marriage. Furthermore, not to commit adultery if they wished to remain married. In any case, faithfulness was required of women and to transgress it amounted to social stigma.

3. Free Ownership, Legacies and Wills

In the third dynasty, Lady Nebesit, mother of the high ranking civil servant Meten, disposed freely of her wealth. She left a will to her children. To her husband she bequeathed fifty aroures (136. 750m). It was understood that all members of the family (father, mother and children) could each own assets and dispose of them the way they saw fit. One can compare this with nineteenth century Victorian England where a married woman's assets automatically became the possession of the husband. Or the reality of Switzerland where a woman, in the twentieth century, did not have the right to vote! One can therefore understand the manacled representations of European women protesting their condition.

In ancient Egypt women were neither under the authority of their husbands nor their eldest sons. Being equal to men in esteem as well as in law, Egyptian women were not under anyone's tutelage. They could inherit from their husbands the same title as their children. The equality in succession rights afforded to sons and daughters, was testimony to the juridical parity between the sexes. Accordingly, like their male counterparts, Egyptian women could acquire real estate. Unlike Mesopotamia, where succession rights for women were limited, Egypt enshrined them into *official policy*.

4. Instruction and Education

As early as the age of four, and for many years, young girls, whose parents, destined to be civil servants, were schooled accordingly. No spectre of caste haunted Egyptian society. Suffice only to recall, as reiterated by Ptah-hotep the sage, that God created all human beings as equal. Thus, Egyptian women from humble background were able — after an appropriate training — to fill posts opened equally to men as well as women. For example, in the sixth dynasty, Lady Nebet, the second mother-in-law of King Pepi 1, was judge and vizier (prime minister). The twenty-sixth dynasty would witness again such an appointment. In the Old Kingdom, some young women were authorised to study medicine and surgery.

Thus, Lady Peseshet, who was buried in a mastaba at Gizeh in the fourth dynasty, was a doctor and held the title of director of female doctors. She was the first known woman doctor in history. Women who studied to become scribes could enter public administration. H. Fisher has recorded more than twenty-five different titles held by women in Pharaonic administration in the Old Kingdom, among which are: supervisor of royal stores, head of department of stores, supervisor of funerary priests, responsible for undertakers.

Lady Nenofer, a landowner and owner of considerable assets in the New Kingdom, had her own business. She was what one might call a true "businesswoman". Indeed, she used to delegate to her commercial agents *(shout you)* the sale of products she wanted to dispose of; her agents had links with their Syrian counterparts.

The clergy itself was open to educated women. By practising cult worship like men they were equally revered and were bestowed with the title of prophets or God's servant *(hemet/neter).* Celibacy was not a prerequisite for service in a temple. The opposite was a later development, after the Egyptian example, of early Christian monks.

Why did women in Egyptian society enjoy such an elevated social, juridical, political, economic and religious position? This question brings us to the very heart of the fundamental "principle" which built Egyptian society.

5. Divine Femininity

Before the universal dawn, the demiurge himself was already both male and female, symbolising thus the fundamental principles: "The fathers and mothers who were with him when he was in the *Noun*" (text of the "Destruction of Men"). This need to identify the female principle in divine action was vital to the inhabitants of *Kemit* (the Black Land). The divine world was conceptualised by Egyptians through images accessible to them and based on the complementarity of the sexes: Noun and Naunet, Hebou and Hehet, (spacial infinity), Amon

and Amonet (hidden entities), Niaou and Niout
(forming the void), Shou (luminous atmosphere) and
Tefnut (humidity), Osiris and Isis, Seth and Nephtys.

Here are extracts from the *Great Hymn to Isis* on a
oxyrihinchos papyrus, number 1380, 1,214 - 216,
second century BC:

Goddess of numerous games,
pride of the female sex,
thou reigneth in the sublime and infinite.

Thou wanteth women (at the age of procreation)
to come and anchor with men
It is thee the mistress of the earth
Thou maketh the power of women equal
to that of men

Thus, the equality between men and women in
Egyptian antiquity was an integral part of the divine
order, as opposed to "economic", "servile",
"ethnographic" or "feudal" considerations. Hence, it
was quite natural for women to be fully integrated
into Pharaonic royalty. The particularly important
role played by the Royal Monarch, great wife of the
king, was maintained throughout the history of Egypt.
Heredity was ensured by the Royal Wife, legitimizer of
all heirs. Upon her fell the duty to transmit the solar
royal blood to the children of the new king. The
rights of the mother, Royal Daughter, were primary.

Over two thousand years ago, the historian Manetho

(third century BC) rightly reminded us that the kings of the second dynasty had established women's complete legitimacy to the throne. How then do we understand "pharaonic mentality"?

Egypt had a universal consciousness of reality which signified an impulsion towards a principle of becoming. And it this becoming which naturally has two primordial elements: male and female. The creative function is fundamental to a universal consciousness. The principle of harmony means that the Egyptians lived in a "cosmic ambiance", and that Egypt is in the image of the sky in its perpetual creation. Thus pharaonic work is a task of constant cosmic renewal.

Therefore, in ancient Egypt:

* *Theology*, religious power, is the doctrine of metaphysical power, and above all, of becoming (*kheper*), of being (*khepri*), of maintaining these principles and of returning to the source;

* *Astronomy* is rightly the science of harmony (*maat*) and of celestial influences;

* *Medicine* is, in Kemit, the dialectical relation of the living body with the cosmic influx and its relation to metaphysical powers — e.g., an Egyptian priest explaining this concept to Solon, in Plato's *Timaeus*.

With such a vision of the world, it is ridiculous to separate the male principle from the female principle, the religious from the political, the economic from the sacred, the clergy from everyday life. Egyptian society was a society of cosmic exaltation, of qualititative exaltation, of spiritualisation. Today, it is difficult to totally understand Pharaonic mentality. So, is it not abusive, indeed erroneous, to use our schemes of sociological analysis to try to understand the social organization of Egypt, which was not simply political/economic, but an organization based on a fundamental cosmic principle which predicated itself on the complementarity of duality!